YOUR EDUCATION MASTERS COMPANION

CW00550988

Your Education Masters Companion will help you choose the ri
needs and provides the essential information you need to pass first time. Offering guidance based on years of experience working with a range of Masters-level students, it unpacks the defining characteristics of successful Masters-level work, and explores key aspects of undertaking your course – reading, writing, producing a literature review, research methodologies, data collection tools, research reports, dissertations and presentations.

What this book will do for you:

- Increase your self-confidence
- Identify the major traps you must avoid if you are to pass your Masters
- Introduce you to the concepts of Masters-level work, what's expected of you and what you can expect from your tutors and supervisors
- Provide guidance on the essential thinking and writing skills that you will need to develop
- Provide guidance on what opportunities are available to you on completion of your Masters.

Your Education Masters Companion is an essential read for any individual thinking about or currently studying for a Masters-level qualification in education.

Jim McGrath was Course Director for the MA in Education and the MA in Education and Professional Development at Birmingham City University, UK.

Anthony Coles works at Birmingham City University, UK, where he is Reader in Post-Compulsory Education and Director of Continuous Professional Development for the Faculty of Education, Law and Social Sciences.

YOUR EDUCATION MASTERS COMPANION

The essential guide to success

Jim McGrath and Anthony Coles

Routledge
Taylor & Francis Group

LONDON AND NEW YORK

First published 2015
by Routledge
2 Park Square, Milton Park, Abingdon, Oxon OX14 4RN

and by Routledge
711 Third Avenue, New York, NY 10017

Routledge is an imprint of the Taylor & Francis Group, an informa business

British Library Cataloguing in Publication Data
A catalogue record for this book is available from the British Library

Library of Congress Cataloging in Publication Data
McGrath, Jim (University lecturer)
Your education masters companion : the essential guide to success / Jim McGrath and Anthony Coles.
pages cm
1. Master of education degree. 2. Universities and colleges–Graduate work.
I. Coles, Anthony. II. Title.
LB1741.5.M45 2015
378.2–dc23
2014046167

ISBN: 978-0-415-73575-9 (hbk)
ISBN: 978-1-408-29594-6 (pbk)
ISBN: 978-1-315-71577-3 (ebk)

Typeset in Interstate
by Swales & Willis Ltd, Exeter, Devon, UK

Printed and bound by CPI Group (UK) Ltd, Croydon, CRO 4YY

In memory of my father Edward 'Alfie' McGrath.

For Bea and William.

CONTENTS

DETAILED CONTENTS

TABLES

HANDOUTS

ABOUT THE AUTHORS

Dr Jim McGrath qualified as an accountant in 1976 and for 20 years worked as an accountant, senior financial manager and management consultant in industry, local government and education. He was Course Director at Birmingham City University for the MA in Education and the MA in Education and Professional Development and taught research skills and management and leadership on a wide range of undergraduate and postgraduate courses.

In 2012 he took early retirement to write full-time and spend more time complaining about his beloved West Bromwich Albion and their limitless ability to always let the faithful down.

Dr Anthony Coles spent his early career as a research chemist before he switched to teaching. He is currently Reader in Post-Compulsory Education and Director of Continuous Professional Development for the Faculty of Education, Law and Social Sciences at Birmingham City University. Much of his work involves research skills and supporting teachers in their professional development.

He has also been responsible for developing links with a number of Chinese universities and establishing the Faculty's MA in International Education and Ed.D. programmes.

Also by the same authors

Your Education Research Project Companion
Your Teacher Training Companion
Your Education Leadership Handbook

INTRODUCTION

How to get the most out of this book

Who is this book for?

This book is for anybody who is thinking about undertaking, or who is currently studying for, a Masters-level qualification in education.

The advice contained in the book is equally applicable to home and overseas students, full- and part-time students, highly capable students and their less-confident students.

The book is a distillation of the knowledge we've gained over 40-plus years working with literally thousands of Masters students. The range of students we have dealt with has been enormous. From the few who failed to pass even one assignment, to the brilliant two or three per cent who we had to run to keep up with. Then there were the many students who started their course believing that they were bound to fail and who ended up gaining an MA with Commendation or Distinction.

People's motives for studying at Masters level vary. Some do it because they need more time to decide on a career. Others for the love of study or as a way to prepare for study at Doctoral level. Most because they believe it will help them advance in their career. One thing that unites them all is a desire to pass the course. That's what this book is about – helping you to choose the right Masters course for your needs and providing the essential information you need to pass the course.

What this book will do for you

- Increase your self-confidence by demonstrating to you that the Masters is just another qualification and that a person of average intelligence can pass provided they work hard.
- Identify the major bear traps you must avoid if you are to pass your Masters.
- Introduce you to the concepts of Masters-level work, what's expected of you and what you can expect from your tutors and supervisors. This knowledge will help you to hit the ground running when you start your course and provide guidance throughout your studies.
- Provide guidance on the essential thinking and writing skills that you will need to develop if you are to succeed at Masters level.
- Provide guidance on what opportunities are available to you on completion of your Masters.

Format and style of the book

The book is divided into ten chapters. Chapters 1-3 deal with the essentials of becoming a Masters student. Chapters 4-5 cover reading, writing and producing a literature review at Masters level. Chapters 6-7 provide a basic introduction to the defining characteristic of Masters-level work, namely research. Chapters 8-9 give advice and guidance on writing five popular types of assignments that are used at Masters level, and Chapter 10 provides advice on what you might do after you have completed your Masters.

Each chapter is broken down into a series of numbered sections. When dealing with something as complex as studying for a Masters, it's not possible to isolate issues to a single chapter or section. By numbering the subsections we can refer you to where you can find additional information about a subject. A full list of these subsections is contained in the Detailed Contents.

The following icons are used throughout the book:

 A large key indicates a **Key Point**.

 A bandaged finger indicates something to **Remember**.

 A thumbs-up figure represents a **Hint**.

 A **Warning** sign denotes something you should beware of/avoid.

The meanings of each should be self-evident. You need to study carefully the Key Points, Remember any reminders, follow the Hints and avoid the Warnings.

As you will see in Chapter 5, it is never sufficient to rely on what one book says about a subject at Masters level. You need to collect the views of other writers. Only then can you weigh up the competing arguments and make an informed decision about who you think presents the most compelling case. This advice also applies to books on how to pass your Masters! We have therefore included suggestions for further reading at the end of each chapter.

One of the things you have to come to terms with quickly at Masters level is the terminology used. Where a term or concept is discussed for the first time it's shown in ***bold italics*** and you will find a definition of the word in the Glossary of Terms at the end of the book.

More generally, you may find the style of the book unusual, especially if you are an overseas student. It lacks formality and even contains the odd joke and funny story. Don't assume that this relaxed, almost light-hearted, style is a sign of sloppy thinking or poor academic practice on our part. It's not. It is a conscious attempt to engage and connect with our readers/students and is based on how we lecture.

In previous books we used Socratic dialogue as a way of teaching research skills and the essential skills and knowledge required by trainee teachers. We did this by structuring each chapter around a meeting between a student and their tutor/mentor/supervisor. That approach was not appropriate for this book. So instead we have modelled each chapter on a lecture. In our opinion the best lecturers are those who tell stories, surprise their listeners by going off on apparent tangents before nailing the point they wish to make and generally keep their students awake and listening by presenting themselves and their materials in an entertaining way. That's what we have aimed to do in this book: to produce a series of chapters/lectures that contain valuable information delivered in a lively and entertaining fashion. As all good lecturers do, we supply you with a handout where we think it will enhance your understanding of the issues discussed.

To maintain the fiction of a lecture, we refer to ourselves as 'I' throughout the book. In addition, we regularly tell you what to do, e.g. 'You should read your final draft assignment aloud'. Some of you may object to what appears as a **didactic** approach to teaching. We want you to pass and if we think that by being directive we can help you pass, that's what we'll do. It's amazing how even great students make the most obvious errors.

How to use the book

Chapter 1 is out of place. Logically it should come at the end of book as it's about the mistakes that Masters students must avoid if they want to be successful. But on the basis that very few students (or lecturers for that matter) read an entire book, we've moved it to the start. The reason is simple. **Avoid these errors and you increase your chances of passing significantly.** Ignore the advice given and you are taking a risk. Of course, if you're a genius you can take risks. But alas, we've not met many geniuses amongst staff or students during our careers so we suggest that you follow the advice we give – until such time as your genius is recognised by all. Even Einstein had to resubmit his Doctoral thesis before it passed.

The remaining chapters are where you would expect to find them. They take you from thinking about doing a Masters course to what you can do after you have completed the course. Don't feel obliged to read every chapter now or to read them in order. Read each chapter as and when it has some meaning for you. If you have already chosen your Masters course you may want to skip Chapter 2 and leave Chapters 6 and 7 until you have learnt something about **research methodology**.

Flipping through the book you will see that it contains a lot of free space. This wasn't done to pad out the book but was part of the design brief that we agreed with Routledge. We want you to use the spaces headed 'Space for your notes' as your **reflective journal**/learning log. So feel free to scribble down any thoughts or ideas that occur to you as you read. Try and turn the book into a personal set of notes. You don't have to spend a lot of time doing this but if you can make a quick note about an issue of interest as you are reading, it will help you to understand and remember what you have read. Such active reading is essential at Masters level (see Chapter 5). You have so much to read and critically evaluate that you need to enter into a dialogue with the literature you use or else you will find yourself just accepting what each writer says as the truth. What you must always remember is 'Truth is never plain or simple' especially in education studies.

We'd like to wish you the best of luck with your studies and to reassure you that all that stands between you and obtaining your Masters is:

- attending the lectures;
- attending seminars and meetings with your tutor/supervisor;
- writing your assignments and dissertation.

There isn't anything magical about it. A Masters requires commitment and perseverance – it does not require an IQ of 150 – although it would probably help.

Jim McGrath
Anthony Coles

Acknowledgements

Jim McGrath would like to acknowledge that the idea for this book came from Anthony.

We would like to thank all the MA students and colleagues whose actions, practices and responses have over many years unwittingly contributed to this book.

We would also like to thank our publisher, Helen Pritt, who has shown unfailing enthusiasm and commitment towards this project. Without you, Helen, the book would never have seen the light of day. Also, Sarah Tuckwell for responding to our queries and keeping us on track.

1 Pass your Masters first time

Ten mistakes to avoid

Aim of chapter: To help you avoid the most common mistakes made by Masters students.

Chapter overview: This chapter outlines ten common mistakes that students make at Masters level. These include failing to use a critical friend, discussing ideas and theories without fully understanding them, lack of self-confidence, and the failure to read widely and take on board feedback provided by markers. Eliminate these errors and your marks will increase substantially.

1.1 Introduction

It may seem odd to start a book on how to gain a Masters-level qualification in education by discussing the mistakes made by students. But it has been situated here for two reasons:

- It will help dispel some of the fears that you may have about studying at Masters level.
- It identifies many of the bear traps that students fall into during their studies and offers some easy ways to avoid them.

Key point: Avoid the errors listed below and you will be well on the way to passing your Masters.

As you read this list you may think, 'Well, that's obvious', which will be a great reaction. Because if you can avoid the errors listed you'll be a long way towards obtaining your Masters. But alas, the problems listed have time after time tripped up even the best students. For example, one excellent student somehow managed to submit an early draft of her dissertation rather than the finished article. Her tutor could only mark what was in front of her and a student who was on track to achieve a Distinction only achieved a bare pass. All because she didn't do a final read-through of her work. An extreme example? Yes. But . . .

The chapter is shorter than many in the book. This is intentional, as many of the issues discussed will be revisited in later chapters.

1.2 The top ten mistakes to avoid

In ascending order of importance, the following are the ten most common mistakes that you should try to avoid.

Starting your assignment too early. This may seem counter-intuitive. For years you have been told by your teachers and lecturers to start your assignments early and to take your time with them. That's not bad advice when you are given the question or topic to write about. But at Masters level you are often required to identify and agree on an assignment title with your tutor/supervisor. Choosing your own title/topic causes many students problems. They are not used to it and are unsure of what an appropriate question or topic would look like. There is also the problem that until you have covered, say, 70 per cent of a module, you are in no position to decide what issues interest you the most or would make the best assignment. So don't be in a rush to start writing. Choose your title when you have completed about three-quarters of the module. As the deadline for submission is probably four or six weeks after the end of the module, this will give you more than enough time to produce your best work.

Delay writing your assignment until the last moment. There are many students who will do anything to avoid starting to write their assignment. They continue to read and take copious notes until their eyes bleed. They plan in precise detail each element of their assignment and make endless cups of tea/coffee and tidy their desk/room until they are working in a dust- and germ-free environment that would be a credit to the Centers for Disease Control and Prevention in Atlanta, Georgia. Anything to avoid starting to write.

You'll know if you suffer from procrastination so use one or both of the following tips to overcome it. First, set a deadline for when you will start writing. When the deadline arrives, sit down and start writing. No excuses. Put your bum on the seat and start writing. Unless you sit down and turn on the computer, you will never write anything. If you find that you can't write, just sit there. Do not get up. Do not do anything else. I think you'll find that within 30 minutes the words will start to flow.

As a general rule of thumb I think you'll need about 20 hours of solid work to write a good 5,000-word assignment. That's about three days' work, but it excludes all the reading, note-taking and research that you may have carried out prior to writing. A 10,000-word assignment may take 45 hours, and a dissertation of more than 20,000 words will take between 75 and 100 hours, or about three weeks of hard work.

Second, remember you don't have to write your assignment in any particular order. Yes, you'll have to present the final effort in specific order, e.g. *abstract*, introduction, literature review, research methodology, findings and *analysis* and conclusions. But you can start anywhere you like. So if you've got great notes from your reading, write the literature review first. If you are fascinated by research methodologies (as a few of us are) start with your research methodology section.

Remember, even professional writers suffer from procrastination, only it's usually multiplied by a factor of ten. Other work and a week in Cornwall have kept me away from writing this book for three weeks. To get back into it I decided to write this section rather than pick up where I had previously left off. Why? Because this area is one that I know students find useful and I'm fascinated by the barriers that stop students achieving. (At the time of writing this I am not at all sure where this chapter will appear in the book. I hope it will appear at the start, but all I can say for certain is that it will appear somewhere.)

Failure to use either a critical friend and/or the university's academic support team (AST). We all have blind spots. Habits that we are unaware of. Such habits extend to our writing and academic work. Mine used to be an utter indifference to apostrophes.

No matter how strong you are academically, there is always the danger that you will fail to recognise some of the weaknesses in your work. All students should find someone on the course that they respect and get on with and agree to act as each other's **critical friend**.

Those students who are worried about their use of English should also contact the university's AST. The support team are generalists, which means that they won't be able to comment on the content of your work, but they will be able to identify grammatical, structural and stylistic problems and offer advice on how to remedy them and improve the clarity and impact of your work.

Failure to carry out a final edit and polish of your assignment before submission. To help you identify errors 'complete' your assignment seven to ten days before the submission deadline. Then put it in a drawer for five days and forget about it. This will give you some much needed distance from the work. Then take it out and read it aloud. This will slow you down and help you read what is actually on the page rather than what you think is/should be there. This process will enable you to identify both the good and bad bits of your assignment. The bad bits you can amend and the good you can enhance further. A final edit like this can help you avoid howlers like: 'I maintained the animosity between all of the research participants'. What the student meant to say was 'I maintained anonymity between the research participants'. Mind you, lecturers do enjoy gaffs like this as it enlivens a long batch of marking.

Failing to understand what good Masters-level writing is all about. Talk about doing a Masters and it conjures up in people's minds the picture of bright, academically gifted students working away on difficult problems in some dusty library or laboratory. Such ideas mean that many students secretly worry that they won't be able to reach the standard required. To compensate, they try to write in what they think is an academic manner and litter their work with big words, jargon and fancy phrasing. The result is that their work lacks clarity and is nearly impossible to read or understand. (Unfortunately there are also some academics who mistakenly believe that writing unintelligible prose is a sign of profundity.)

Clarity is more important than style. Let me say that again. **CLARITY IS MORE IMPORTANT THAN STYLE**. What you must aim for is clear, simple, sharp English that helps the reader to understand your arguments. If you have a choice between using a big word and a small one always choose the smaller option. Of course, there will be times when it is appropriate to use big words or jargon, as only a specific word or phrase will do the job, but seek to minimise them.

 Remember: 'Great art is the expression of complex ideas in a simple form' (Albert Einstein). At Masters level you have to express complex ideas in a clear and simple way. Don't try to be clever.

Linked to the problem of big words is using words or phrases that you don't fully understand. Don't advertise how desperate you are to impress by using words, phrases and jargon that you don't fully understand. It smacks of the young child trying to join in with the big kids and getting the language all wrong or lecturers trying to talk to students using what they think is the latest slang.

SPACE FOR YOUR NOTES

Never discuss an idea or theory that you don't fully understand. Unless you fully understand an idea you can't write convincingly about it and your lack of understanding will quickly become apparent to your reader. Such an 'error' advertises your weaknesses and undermines your credibility. This affects how your tutor reads the rest of your assignment and colours their thinking about your work. So avoid it.

Not reading widely enough. When you start to study a module at Masters level you may or may not know what your assignment will be about. But you can't leave your reading until you decide. You need to adopt a two-stage *reading strategy*.

In Stage One you start reading immediately. You do this to gain the depth of knowledge required to produce a good assignment. Using any references your lecturer gives you in the sessions and the recommended reading list for the course, follow up the topics discussed in each session. At this stage don't worry about taking too many notes – just read to increase your general understanding of the subject.

When you have identified a title or topic for your assignment you enter Stage Two. It is now that you revisit those books and articles that you previously read which are relevant to your work and undertake a proper literature search to find material that deals specifically with the issues you wish to explore. It is at this point that you start to take detailed notes and build up your *theoretical framework* (see Chapter 5).

It is the literature that you access in Stage Two that you use in your assignment. Why then, you might ask, is Stage One reading so important? The basic reading that you do in Stage One increases your knowledge of the subject, enables you to make an informed choice of assignment and establishes in your brain ideas and theories which enrich your thinking about the subject generally. This knowledge, which is often held subconsciously, enables you to critically evaluate and discuss the key literature you use in your assignment at a depth of understanding which is not available to those who skipped Stage One.

As an experienced marker of MA assignments I can always distinguish between those students who have read widely and those who have only accessed the books which appear in the list of references. How? Simple. Those who have read widely think and write like someone who has mastery of their subject in everything they write.

Failing to discuss your assignment with your tutor or supervisor. There really is no excuse not to discuss your assignment with your tutor or supervisor. Yet many students never approach them for help or advice. Occasionally such students are brilliant mavericks and turn out wonderful work, but for us poor mortals such an approach is likely to lead to disaster and a resit.

Warning: Failure to make use of the skills, knowledge and academic experience of your tutors and supervisors will in 99.9 per cent of cases lead to a disappointing outcome.

If you are writing an assignment you may or may not get formal tutorial support, i.e. a specific allocation of time with your tutor to discuss your assignment. Arrangements vary from university to university. But even where no formal time allocation is made, at a minimum, always agree with your tutor the following:

- the title of your assignment;
- an outline to the main issues that you intend to address in the assignment;
- the key texts that you will use;
- details of how you will collect any ***primary data*** that you will use (see Chapter 7).

You could even summarise these points on a single sheet of paper and give it to your tutor for comments and suggestions. I don't know of any lecturer who would fail to respond to such a request. After all, it's in their interest that you pass. If you fail it reflects badly on them and they have to provide you with additional support and mark your resubmission.

If you are doing a piece of research you will almost certainly be allocated a supervisor who will guide you through the research process. They will have allocated on their teaching timetable a number of hours for each research student. This time allocation includes the time they take to read what you write as you develop your research project or dissertation and to meet with you face to face.

Don't be passive in these meetings. Take with you a list of queries/questions/worries that you have and make sure that you get an answer to each before you leave. Lecturers love to supervise students who are proactive and organised.

Hint: Always record your supervision sessions. Your supervisor will want you to discuss what you are currently doing, what you plan to do and the progress you are making on the work. They will also want to challenge and query your ideas and the research approach you've chosen. With all that going on you won't have the time to take accurate notes.

Failing to turn up. Edison said that genius was '1 per cent inspiration and 99 per cent perspiration', while Woody Allen suggested that '95 per cent of success is turning up'.

Studying for a Masters, especially as a part-time or overseas student, can be a lonely affair. The only people who can appreciate what you are going through are your fellow students and, to a lesser extent, your tutor. So turn up to every taught session and tutorial. Regular attendance will provide the structure and support you need to keep going. It's doubly important to attend when things are going badly at home or work. Even if you can't do any reading or start collecting data because of other commitments, use the sessions as an escape from the pressures of your life; as some 'me time' – an area of calm in your life over which you have significant control.

If you miss one session it's not a disaster. But miss two and you are starting to fall behind your colleagues. Miss three or four and you are in danger of becoming detached from the course. More than that and it's very unlikely that you will ever return.

Taught sessions and tutorials guide you through the module and are used by lecturers to highlight the important elements of the course. In addition they will usually contain a lot of 'process information', e.g. when, where and how you should submit your assignments, including rules about referencing and *plagiarism* as well as opportunities to present your assignment ideas to the group and receive feedback. Such information and support can't be obtained from a textbook.

The group will keep you going. If you're competitive, you won't want to be beaten by your colleagues. If you are uncertain, you'll benefit from their support and advice. Most of all, the group will show you that how you feel and the problems you are encountering are shared by many, if not all, in the group.

Even apparently negative *feedback* from the group can be useful. On the first night of my MA in Education the tutor went around the room asking each student to sketch in their professional background. When it came to me I explained that I was not a teacher and had only recently moved into the education sector in a management capacity. When I'd finished, the woman next to me, who had been a lecturer in Further Education for many years, leaned across and said, 'You're going to find this course difficult'. It was at that point that I decided I would complete and pass the course. Which is exactly what I did. The moral of this story – use whatever the group offers to motivate yourself.

Lack of self-confidence. Ultimately the biggest mistake that many students make is to believe that they are not good enough to pass the course. They feel like an imposter and that they don't belong on a Masters course – after all, they aren't an academic. Ironically, it is often these students, the ones with genuine self-doubt, who excel once they get into the course and receive feedback on their first assignment.

Lack of confidence can often result in non-submission of an assignment and fulfilment of the student's own self-fulfilling prophecy – namely failure. The truth is that the pass rates on most Masters programmes are very high. The figures in Table 1.1 are based on results from a *new university*, whose MA in various education programmes enjoys an excellent reputation.

Table 1.1   Masters degree results

Masters degree results	%
Pass with Distinction	12
Pass/Pass with Commendation	78
Fail	10

Of the 10 per cent who fail, seven out of ten fail because they didn't submit their assignment. This means that only about 3 per cent of students who submit an assignment actually fail. The others failed because they were too afraid or too lazy to try.

 Remember: Most people suffer from the imposter syndrome, which means that they don't believe they are bright enough to be on a Masters programme and it's only a matter of time before their tutor finds out and asks them to leave. Even so, 90 per cent-plus overcome these doubts and submit an assignment. You must do the same. Only you can find the courage and self-confidence to succeed.

1.3 Conclusion

Many years ago I ran a course for managers on interviewing technique. Trying to liven up things after a particularly heavy lunch for all concerned, I decided to risk a new approach. Instead of role playing how to conduct a great interview, I decided to show what being interviewed by the world's worst interviewer would be like. I didn't tell the group what I was going to do but I did share it with the volunteer who I was interviewing.

Initially there was confusion, then titters, and finally outright laughter as the group caught on to what I was doing. Afterwards, I debriefed the group, asking them what I had done wrong. Their list was extensive and included a few items that I hadn't picked up on. It was then that I made the point. If they avoided all the mistakes that I'd made the chances were that they would conduct an effective interview.

That's why I've started this book with mistakes to avoid. Avoid the above errors and you stand every chance of being successful in your Masters studies.

SPACE FOR YOUR NOTES

Further reading

McGivney, V. (1993) Participation and Non-Participation: A Review of the Literature, in Edwards, R., Sieminski, S. and Zeldin, D. (Eds) *Adult Learners, Education and Training: A Reader*. London: Routledge/OUP.

2   What's involved in doing a Masters

> **Aim of chapter:** To provide an introduction to the world of Masters-level study.
>
> **Chapter overview:** This chapter explores the reasons why people undertake a Masters course and the benefits that flow from successful completion. Advice is given on the numerous Masters-level qualifications that are now available and the practical considerations that students must take into account before selecting a course. An outline of the Qualifications and Credit Framework descriptors at level 7 is also provided.

2.1 Introduction

 Key point: You need to identify exactly why you want to study for a Masters and what you expect to get out of it before you start. Such clarity will keep you motivated when the going gets tough.

Fifty years ago only 10 per cent of the population went to university to study for an undergraduate degree. Therefore, it was not surprising that only a tiny proportion of the population went on to study for a Masters. Masters tended to be the preserve of academics and those whose occupations required a deep understanding of a specific area of knowledge, such as lawyers, researchers and university lecturers.

This has changed significantly in the last 20 years with most professional bodies now encouraging their members to continue their studies after qualification. This has become possible because of the number of postgraduate, part-time and distance learning courses at Masters level that are now available. Today's would-be Masters student is faced with a bewildering array of courses to choose from.

This chapter provides you with an introduction to the range of courses that are available in the education field and raises a series of issues that you need to consider before choosing your course.

2.2 Reasons to study for a Masters

 Hint: I'm sure that you've asked yourself the question 'Why do I want a Masters degree?' and if you haven't, your friends and family probably have. If asked at a job interview why you are doing a Masters tell them what they want to hear, i.e. 'Because I think it will improve my professional practice/performance'.

If asked the question at a university interview you might say, 'For the love of learning, to stretch myself, to study something I love in greater depth or to improve my professional performance/practice'. All are valid reasons, and aspects of them may play a part in your decision. But when the going gets tough, and it will, you need something more substantial to keep you writing and reading long into the night.

Teachers, lecturers and trainers are practical, busy people. The following is a list of the practical advantages that having a Masters degree will provide:

- **A competitive advantage** when you apply for a job. When faced with 20 candidates, all of whom meet the essential and desirable criteria listed in the person specification, a Masters will help you stand out from the crowd and secure an interview.
- **The qualification you may need to gain promotion.** Many Masters programmes contain a module on management and/or leadership. A good understanding of these will be essential if you wish to step into management.
- **To prepare you for entry on to a Ph.D. course.** In truth nothing can prepare you adequately for the step up to Doctoral study. However, the experience of undertaking primary and *secondary research* at Masters level will be very useful.
- **An opportunity to improve your professional practice** and your professional reputation, both of which are essential if you wish to be promoted within your existing school or when applying for a job externally.
- **Improve your thinking skills for life.** Long after you have forgotten the content of the modules you studied, you will retain vital transferrable skills, such as improved critical thinking, increased evaluation skills, an ability to understand and explain complex issues clearly and research skills that can be applied in a wide range of situations. The more effort you put into your Masters the greater the growth will be. I have known students who changed their career, set up their own business or emigrated following successful completion of their Masters.

Remember: Masters-level work is as much about developing your transferable and employability skills as gaining the qualification.

2.3 Personal development and studying for a Masters

Any person who undertakes a Masters can expect to see a degree of personal development which will remain with them for life. These may include, but aren't limited to, the skills and knowledge listed in Table 2.1. How significant your development will be is entirely down to you. The more effort you put into your studies the greater personal growth you can expect.

In addition to the above benefits, you also get to put MA after your name, which I've found impresses the hell out of people who don't work in education and some that do. But, unlike me, I'm sure you're not into such self-aggrandisement. Are you?

Remember: What you get out of your Masters is entirely dependent on how much effort you put into your studies.

Table 2.1   Personal development benefits you gain from doing a Masters

- A body of expert knowledge, including the current theories that are popular in your area of work.
- The skills necessary to carry out a small-scale piece of research.
- An ability to critically evaluate both the theories currently advocated in your area of study and the data you collect.
- Improved analytical skills.
- An appreciation of how all theories are just a partial explanation of a complex reality and may change as new data is discovered.
- An understanding of how both the theory and practice of education is constantly changing and the ability to evaluate those changes.
- An ability to critically evaluate proposed changes in the workplace before they are implemented.
- An understanding of the effect that government policy, including inspection, has on teaching.
- An ability to think for yourself and to act as an autonomous learner.
- The skills, knowledge and self-confidence required to actively manage your career, whether that entails seeking promotion, changing employers or further study.
- Improved writing skills.
- Greater self-awareness, as many of your existing ideas and beliefs will be challenged.

SPACE FOR YOUR NOTES

2.4 Qualifications available at Masters level

The Masters degree used to confer on its holder the right to teach. Effectively, it said that the holder was 'a master of their subject'. This gave rise to the old description of a teacher as a Master. At one time you either studied for a Master of Art (MA) or a Master of Science (M.Sc.). Now there is a plethora of qualifications and you need to ensure that you choose the course which is right for your needs and aspirations.

The following is a list of the most common Masters-level qualifications that are available today:

Warning: Not all Masters programmes are the same. Identify what you need, the constraints you face in terms of time, finances and study opportunities and then choose your Masters programme. Be realistic.

Recognised programmes of study leading to a full Masters qualification:

- Master of Business Administration (MBA) in Education Management and Leadership
- Masters in Teaching and Learning (MTL)
- Masters in Teaching (M.Teach)
- Master of Arts in Education (MA Education)
- Master of Philosophy (M.Phil.)

Which qualification you settle on will depend on your circumstances and what you want to do when qualified. The nature of the programme may not be the only reason for your choice. The location and time of the course, entry requirements, ease of reaching the university, study methods and cost may be some of the other factors that will influence your decision.

 Hint: Masters courses, even with the same title, often vary significantly in terms of approach, content and style. Use the normally excellent web sites provided by universities to understand what's on offer.

PGCE: With some or all modules at Masters level

A Masters degree does **not** provide the holder with a teaching qualification - *qualified teacher status (QTS)* - in England and Wales. Every year, when interviewing candidates for the Masters programme I found one or two people who were convinced that a Masters degree would enable them to teach in a school or college. It doesn't - not in England and Wales.

If you wish to qualify as a teacher you should either do an undergraduate teacher training course which carries qualified teacher status or, if you already have a first degree, look at doing a Postgraduate Certificate in Education (PGCE) or signing up for one of the many other routes into education, such as Schools Direct or Teach First.

If you are a trainee teacher looking for a PGCE course and have a long-term ambition to obtain a Masters degree, study for a PGCE that offers all modules at Masters level. Universities that offer such PGCEs usually allow graduates to claim credit for the 120 credits they have earned against one or more of their Masters courses. This means that following your PGCE you will only have to complete a dissertation to obtain your Masters degree.

Courses that can contribute to a full Masters qualification:

- PGCE 120 credits with a mixture of level 6 and 7 modules
- PGCE 120 credits with all modules at Masters level

Master of Business Administration (MBA) in Education Management

MBAs are usually considerably more expensive than other postgraduate degrees. This extra cost is meant to reflect the additional cachet that the title provides. However, not all MBAs are equal. It is a fact that where you do your MBA defines the value that students and employers place upon it. An MBA from Harvard or Oxford is extremely valuable, not because the content and standard of the course is better than that offered by many **red brick universities**, but because of the network of contacts that it provides to every student on the course: a network that spreads across the world and into numerous boardrooms and government offices. If you are doing your MBA in Education and Leadership at a new university you will probably pay considerably more than for a standard Masters course but not enjoy the same network of contacts as your peers at Oxford.

Masters in Teaching and Learning (MTL) and M.Teach

The Masters in Teaching and Learning (MTL) and the Masters in Teaching (M.Teach) share many similarities. Both are concerned with exploring and improving the individual's professional practice. This means there is a focus on practice-based research, such as teaching and learning issues or subject specialisms and how this form of **critical evaluation** and research activity can improve the individual's classroom practice. A strong emphasis is placed on the need for students to disseminate their findings to peers in their school with the intention of improving overall school performance.

M.Teach programmes can be run either in partnership with a school or as a separate stand-alone programme at a university, whereas the MTL is run as a partnership between a school or college and a university. To join either course you will need to be employed in a suitable education setting. This means that these courses are not suitable for overseas students.

 Hint: If your school offers either the MTL or M.Teach, grab it with both hands. It's nearly always free. You can do part of the course in works time and it's convenient. It will also set you on the road to promotion within your school.

Master of Arts in Education (MA in Education)

This is a traditional Masters programme, which may have a focus on practice, but could alternatively have a more theoretical orientation. The traditional MA is popular with both home and overseas students. However, do check if it is practice-based as this can present problems to full-time home and overseas students who don't have access to an educational environment in which to undertake their research.

An MA in Education tends to be university-based, but some universities run modules within schools and colleges. However, although school-based mentors may attend such sessions, the programmes are normally taught by university staff.

In a world that increasingly values specialism, the MA prefix has been added to a wide range of specialist qualifications, including MA In Education Management and Leadership, MA in International Management, MA in Education and Professional Development, MA in Distance Learning and MA in Higher Education.

One other qualification that has evolved from the MA in Education is the Masters in Education (M.Ed.). This qualification shares many characteristics with the MA but does not generally require students to undertake an extended research project in the form of a dissertation. Instead, emphasis is placed on taught modules.

Hint: Along with the M.Phil, the MA in Education (or whatever suffix you wish to append to it) probably enjoys the highest level of recognition among educationalists. If you intend to work as a teacher, lecturer or trainer this is probably the best course to take – particularly if you are an overseas student as the MA qualification is held in very high regard worldwide.

Master of Philosophy (M.Phil.)

An M.Phil., or Master of Philosophy, is essentially a research degree similar to a Ph.D. but shorter and at a lower level. It usually involves a minimum of one year's full-time study or two years part-time. A university-based supervisory team is appointed and you will find yourself working alone for much of the course as you pursue your own research interests. There will be occasions when you meet other M.Phil., Ed.D. and Ph.D. students, for example, at the joint research training sessions or when you present your research to other colleagues and tutors. However, the degree tends to be very much an individual effort and there is little group support for you to fall back on. For that reason you can feel quite isolated.

Unlike most other Masters qualifications, which tend to be assessed using a mixture of assignments, projects and a dissertation, the M.Phil. is assessed on one 40,000–50,000-word thesis which you will have to defend at a *viva voce* before two examiners. The Internal Examiner will be appointed from within the university, but they will have played no part in your teaching or supervision. The other, known as the External, will be appointed from another university. Both examiners will be familiar with your area of work and you can expect a supportive but challenging examination which can last up to an hour and a half.

The number of topics you can research at M.Phil. is very wide, limited only by the expertise/ research interests of the university's staff. You will be required to *focus* your research on a small area of work and examine it in significant depth. Your research may or may not be practice-based.

Hint: If your ultimate ambition is to study for a Ph.D. then I would recommend you study for an M.Phil. The M.Phil. process mirrors much more closely life on the Ph.D. than any other Masters-level qualification. It also enjoys a high reputation amongst educationalists, and if you make satisfactory progress you may be able to transfer on to the Ph.D. programme and continue your studies as a Doctoral student.

SPACE FOR YOUR NOTES

2.5 Practical considerations when choosing your course

The readers of this book include home, overseas, full- and part-time students, able-bodied and the disabled. Therefore, the range of practical considerations that readers may need to consider are virtually limitless. Only you will know your own unique situation. Use the following as a starting point for compiling your own unique list.

Entry requirements. The top universities – Oxford, Cambridge and other *Russell Group universities* – will require a First, or at the very minimum, a 2:1 undergraduate degree or equivalent. Other universities may accept a 2:2 degree as an entry qualification, and for mature students the academic requirement may be waived and instead they will be asked to demonstrate how they might contribute to and benefit from studying at Masters level. From experience, I know that many of the most able and successful students were the mature students who had few or no academic qualifications but a huge desire to succeed.

In addition to the above, overseas students will have to demonstrate proficiency in English by meeting the appropriate level of proficiency in the International English Language Testing System (IELTS). Normally this is set at 6.5. However, I would urge all overseas students to try and improve on this figure before they arrive in the UK, as poor written skills are often the biggest problem faced by students from abroad.

Cost of course. Fees vary considerably between universities. Therefore you need to shop around. Don't automatically assume that the universities with the highest prices are beyond your means. Some offer a reduction for students paying their own fees and/or can provide financial support through scholarships and private grants. So inquire. In addition, check out if the university allows you to pay by instalments.

Funding your studies. We'd all like to go to Harvard, Oxford or Cambridge to study, but even if we meet the required entry requirements we may not be able to afford to study at these great universities. Your first step in funding your studies is finding out how much they will cost. Once you have an idea of how much it will cost, you can consider how you will fund your studies. Sources of funding available to you include:

- self-financed from savings or loan;
- self-financed from earnings (note there are restrictions on the number of hours overseas students can work when studying full-time);
- financed by partner or parents;
- fees paid by employer;
- grants (not available in UK but may be available to overseas students);
- scholarships.

At the interview stage discuss what financial support, if any, the university can offer and be prepared to fund your studies from multiple sources. They will also have details of any scholarships that you might be able to apply for.

Part-time students often find it difficult to obtain funding from their school or college for their MA studies. School managers can fail to see the benefits that such a course brings to the organisation. This is a misunderstanding of the nature of the programme. Most universities will encourage you to study issues that are relevant to your own professional practice, and you can use what you learn from taught modules and your own research to explore and resolve school-based problems. Many students I've taught on the MA were able to base all their assignments around live issues in their school. In fact, they were encouraged to do just that. This brought enormous benefits to their school in the long run. All students should use these arguments with their employers and governments when seeking financial support.

The academic standing of the university you have chosen. It's not sufficient to choose the best university you can get into. You need to examine the faculty of education's performance within the university. Many new universities have education faculties that are the equal of any red brick university because they were previously a teacher training college. Check out *The Sunday Times Good University Guide*, published annually and accessible online, to identify the best faculties/schools of education.

Accommodation cost, availability and location. As a postgraduate student you may not wish to live in halls of residence composed of first-year undergraduates who are exploring the limits of their freedom now that they have been released from all parental control. As a general rule, accommodation and living expenses reduce the further north you go, and by the same token London is by some way the most expensive place to study. But it's got the theatres, the clubs, the concerts and a thousand and one other attractions – most of which the average student can't afford to access!

Ease of travel to and from the university and from the university to your family home. A long journey to and from university on a bitterly cold winter's morning can persuade even the most conscientious student to stay in bed. So avoid excessively long journeys and the need to change trains/buses.

If you have moved from your home town or country to study, you also need to consider how easy it will be for you to get home should an emergency occur.

Level of student support offered by the university. There are two areas of support that you might need to access: academic and pastoral. Most universities offer a range of academic support for students, everything from courses on how to reference materials to writing dissertations. Pastoral care is about looking after the non-academic needs of students. This is an area that is particularly important for full-time and overseas students. Hopefully you will never need to access pastoral support, but if a death in the family or serious illness strikes it can be the difference between completing your course and leaving.

What's the nature of the course? If you read 2.4 above you will see that some courses effectively require you to be working in an education or training environment, otherwise you will be unable to complete the practice-based assignments, e.g. the MTL. Others, such as the M.Ed., MA and M.Phil. can be based upon a more academic tradition. These qualifications may allow you to complete the course using only **secondary data** which would not require you to have access to an education organisation.

If you are an overseas student, or a home-based student studying full-time, you should confirm the nature of the assignments and **research** that they will expect you to undertake. If they expect you to carry out **empirical research** and collect primary data you will find it extremely difficult to complete your assignments, as access to schools and colleges will require you to undergo a Criminal Records Bureau (CRB) check. For an overseas student it can take six months to obtain a CRB certificate, as checks will have to be made in your country of origin.

Accreditation of Prior Learning (APL) is an umbrella term for the process by which universities and colleges of higher education give credit against learning previously achieved by an individual. The term includes both Accreditation of Prior Certificated Learning (APCL) and Accreditation of Prior Experiential Learning (APEL).

An APCL recognises a student's previous learning which has been assessed and certificated by an education provider (for example, by another university or professional body).

APEL relates to the recognition of learning that a student may have acquired outside a formal education and training system. For example, you may have written a report at work for management. With suitable amendment, such as adding a literature review, you may be able to submit it for APEL.

Students can make a claim for advance standing based upon either APCL or APEL. The rules for claiming both vary between universities and you should read the university's policy on APL before you are interviewed, at which time you can seek clarification for anything you don't understand.

The advantage of APL is that it can reduce the number of modules you have to sit, the time it takes to obtain the qualification and the costs of your course. So it's worth exploring.

Remember: The M.Ed. and MA in Education are the most suitable courses for overseas students. But make sure that all assignments can be completed without the need for empirical research.

SPACE FOR YOUR NOTES

2.6 The Qualifications and Credit Framework

This section is included here because at some time in your deliberations you have to ask yourself the question 'Am I up to studying for a Masters qualification?' I can tell you now that if you have ever taught in a classroom then you have already demonstrated many of the **standards** outlined below in your daily work. As a teacher you've had to exercise decision-making skills in complex situations, for example, when dealing with a disruptive learner whose conduct is causing problems. In solving the problem you would have had to analyse a complex situation and select the best course of action (decision-making skills) from the wide range of alternatives available.

 Warning: So stop worrying about the standards. You are up to studying for and passing a Masters. The question you should really ask is 'Am I willing to work hard enough to reach the required academic standard to pass the course?' If you aren't committed to working hard over the entire length of the course, give up now and save your money. Because 'good enough work' is never good enough at Masters level.

Universities in England, Wales and Northern Ireland operate under what is known as the Qualifications and Credit Framework (QCF). There are eight levels, of which the final five relate to university-level study (see Table 2.2).

As you would expect, the standard of difficulty increases as you progress through the levels. However, it's fair to say that from level 4 to 7 the increase between each is something of a gentle slope. Yes, your work is judged against a higher standard, but it is not a particularly huge step up to the new level. All that's required is that you work conscientiously and consistently over the period of your course and you'll very likely pass. This is not true of the step up from level 7 to level 8, where the gap is very significant as implied by the shaded line in Table 2.2.

 Warning: If you are taking a Masters as preparation for Doctoral study don't expect it to prepare you for the shock of level 8 work. It is a genuine culture shock.

Table 2.3 summarises the level 7 standards that you will have to meet at Masters level.

Table 2.2   Qualifications and Credit Framework: levels 4 to 8

Level	Description
4	First-year undergraduate
5	Second-year undergraduate
6	Third-year undergraduate
7	Masters
8	Doctorate

Table 2.3   Qualifications and Credit Framework: level descriptors

Under the heading Intellectual Skills and Attributes you are required to:

- Display your mastery of a complex area of specialist knowledge and/or skills. The keyword here is *mastery*. You have to convince the examiner that you fully understand your area of study.
- Demonstrate expertise in your use and knowledge of advanced and highly specialised technical, professional and/or research skills. The keyword here is *expertise*. It's not enough to use the skills; you must demonstrate a high level of skill in their use.

Under the heading Process you must be able to:

- Conduct research, or advanced technical or professional activity, using and adapting your skills and the tools available to you to suit the demands of the task you are engaged in.
- Design and apply a research methodology that is appropriate to your project. This is why it's so important that you fully justify your choice of research methodology and demonstrate why it was the best approach to adopt for your research (see 6.12 and 7.8).
- Provide evidence that you have, or intend to, disseminate your findings to peers and/or other researchers. This can often be achieved by presentations to fellow students and/or tutors.
- Develop new skills to a high level, including the mastery of new techniques and ideas.
- Work in a wide range of professional contexts which are inherently unpredictable.

Under the heading Accountability you must:

- Willingly accept that you are accountable for the decisions you make during your research, including how you have used feedback given to you by supervisors.
- Take responsibility for the work of other professional staff who report to you, and lead and initiate activities where appropriate.

(Adapted from Qualifications and Credit Framework)

Hint: Use my notes above to gain an understanding of the standards you are expected to achieve. Then access www.gov.uk/what-different-qualification-levels-mean/overview and refer to the 'Compare different qualification levels' web page. This page contains the official definitions of the standards you will be required to meet.

Warning: As you study the standards ask yourself 'Am I willing to put the work in that is required?' Only you can answer that question, and you need to do it honestly before you spend a lot of time and money on a course that you'll never complete.

2.7 Assignment criteria

Working at Masters level is all about depth not breadth of knowledge. While the Qualifications and Credit Framework sets the standards at which you must operate at to pass a Masters-level qualification, the actual criteria against which each piece of work will be assessed is set by your university/tutor. Normally you will be given a copy of the criteria for each assignment that you are required to submit. A copy of the criteria should also appear in either the student handbook or module handbook, both of which will be available on your university's intranet.

The module criteria will typically list four or five criteria that you have to pass. The descriptors for each criterion are normally subdivided into categories such as Fail, Pass, Good Pass, Commendation and Distinction. When marking your assignment each criterion is marked separately. In some universities you will have to pass every criterion in order to pass. In others you can fail a criterion, but provided your averaged score exceeds the pass mark for the module (usually 50 per cent) you are awarded a pass. For example, say there are five criteria and each attracts 20 per cent of the total marks available. You could score 15 per cent, 12 per cent, 8 per cent, 14 per cent and 13 per cent, giving you a total of 62 per cent – a clear Pass and probably a Commendation, even though you failed to score 50 per cent of the marks available in one of the criterion, i.e. 8/20 x 100 = 40 per cent. Check which system of marking your university uses.

2.8 Time commitment required

This section is about the time you must be willing to devote to your studies, not time management; for that see Sections 3.4 and 3.5.

The 'gold standard' in terms of study at Masters level is 5 hours personal study for each hour spent in class. So for a 30-hour module you'd be expected to do personal reading amounting to 150 hours. This figure excludes any actual research that you undertake and the time required to write your assignment.

Personally, I think you are looking at 20 hours of study per week for each 30-credit module if you are a full-time student, and 10 hours per week if you are a part-time student. Unfortunately, averages aren't much use because inevitably you will work twice as hard/long when actively working on your assignment.

 Hint: Beware of good intentions. It's all right you saying that you'll commit X hours a week to your studies, but how realistic is that? Based on past performance, how many hours per week did you spend in private study on your last major qualification/course? Be honest. There is no one watching you or judging you. That figure is a much better guide to how long you are likely to devote to your Masters studies than any well-intentioned timetable/plan. **If you can't do the time don't do the course!**

2.9 Conclusion

This chapter deals with mundane issues. However, they are important and if possible you should discuss them with someone you trust before turning up for your MA interview (Skype is increasingly used for interviewing overseas students).

Studying for a Masters is not something to be done on a whim. It's a major decision, so take your time. Consider carefully your options and the implications that flow from any decision you make. Then, if you decide to go for it, put all your efforts into the programme. Don't be half-hearted. Pursue your objective with real energy and commitment. Do that and you'll enjoy a great learning experience.

SPACE FOR YOUR NOTES

Further reading

'Compare different qualifications', <www.gov.uk/what-different-qualification-levels-mean/overview>, then refer to the page 'Compare different qualification levels'. (Accessed 1 February 2015)

3 Becoming a Masters student

Aim of chapter: To enable you to make the transition from undergraduate student to autonomous postgraduate learner.

Chapter overview: This chapter explores what it means to be an ***autonomous learner*** and to act like a professional and committed student. Responsibilities inherent in these terms include accepting personal responsibility for work submitted, meeting deadlines and using feedback to enhance future performance. To assist learners, a range of time-saving strategies are outlined, and advice on how to maximise the outputs from every learning session is given.

3.1 Introduction

 Key point: All Masters courses are underpinned by an element of either primary or secondary research. Only you can do that research. Therefore, you must take responsibility for your studies.

This chapter is about how to become a Masters student. You'll be happy to know that you don't have to undergo any mystical initiation ceremony or trek 38 miles over the Brecon Beacons in less than 8 hours. But you do need to rethink your role as a student.

At undergraduate level there is a clear power relationship between tutor and student, with the tutor the dominant personality in the relationship. A good relationship at Masters level should be based on partnership not power. At the start of the course you are the junior partner but by the end you have progressed to near equality with your tutor (full equality is reached should you pursue a doctorate).

The transition is not always easy. It requires you to become more professional about your studies and take responsibility for your own actions, learning and outcomes. The chapter starts by looking at what it means to be an autonomous learner before exploring the bare minimum that is expected of you as a Masters student. It ends by exploring how you can save and manage that most precious of commodities – time.

3.2 Becoming an autonomous learner

Let me start by recognising that some of you may already be autonomous learners. However, it's a sad reflection on many British schools and universities that they continue to turn out students and graduates who have wonderful memories but lack the ability to analyse and critically evaluate data and information for themselves. This problem is not confined to Britain and is actually worse in countries where education is tightly controlled by a small elite.

Key point: As a postgraduate student you must take responsibility for your own learning. You cannot expect your tutors to spot that you are having difficulties and step in to help. Nor can you expect them to spoon-feed you or run around checking that you've handed in your latest assignment.

You're a mature person who has to take responsibility for your own actions, and that includes learning. If you run into a problem with your studies it's you who has to take action to resolve it. That action may involve approaching your tutor for advice and/or support, but it's up to you to take the initiative.

For most of your educational career you've been told what to do, when to do it, what to read and write and, to some degree, what to think. You've been rewarded for doing what your teachers and tutors have told you. Breaking away from this paternalistic culture and standing on your own two academic feet and thinking for yourself doesn't happen overnight. Nor does it occur because of one single change that you make. Rather, it's the culmination of numerous small changes in attitude and behaviour which turns you into an independent-minded person capable of thinking through positions and issues for yourself, sifting the evidence and arriving at your conclusion about what is going on and not just accepting the views of other writers, students, commentators or lecturers.

 Warning: Independence of thought is not about making strident statements. For example, if you were asked to say what you thought of Shakespeare's *Macbeth* it would not be sufficient to say, 'I thought the play was rubbish'. You'd need to explain and justify with reference to other commentators why the play was rubbish (see 4.2).

The advice given in this chapter will help you to start the process. The strategy outlined for how you can bring about this change is not rocket science or even brain surgery (should that be the other way around? Which really is the harder?) – mostly it's just common sense.

 Remember: Don't just read what your lecturer recommends or accept what they say. That's their opinion/position. Your lecturer is as biased as any other commentator.

One thing that annoys me greatly is to see MA and Ph.D. students become clones of their supervisors, voicing their tutor's views and opinions as if they were their own. That's what I call a waste of an expensive education. Read, think and develop your own views – don't become a cipher for someone else's opinions.

3.3 Becoming a professional student

 Key point: If you want to be a Masters student, act like a Masters student, and pretty soon you'll become one.

Act professionally to become professional. As in so much of these early chapters you may think that what is discussed in this chapter is obvious. However, the number of students who fail to act in a professional manner are legion. This was summed up by one student whose dissertation I failed. He sought me out and told me that, 'You can't fail me. I'm not like other students on this course. I paid for it with my own money'.

So how do professional students act? You start with self-confidence.

Self-confidence. As in so much of life, confidence is the key to success. You can't become an autonomous learner if you lack self-confidence; you'll always be looking for someone to validate your views/actions. Therefore, from day one think, act and behave like a Masters student. Especially if you are suffering from the world's worst case of imposter syndrome (see 1.2). Act confident and you will become confident. Put yourself in uncomfortable positions, e.g. making presentations, asking questions in class and arguing for your point of view with your tutor. Pretty soon you'll wonder why you ever found such tasks difficult/ frightening.

Record sessions. At the start of the course arrange with your tutors to record their sessions. I don't suggest that you make a full transcription of these recording notes at a later stage, as transcribing an hour of speech can take around four hours depending on how fast you type. But it's a sad fact that after a week a good student will only remember 30 per cent of the lecture. Listen to the same lecture again within a week and that figure increases to about 70 per cent.

Take notes. Even if you are recording the session take brief notes of the key points raised in the session. They will act as a memory jogger and a 'table of contents' for the session, which will help you find material you are looking for when you are writing your assignments. Keep the recording until you finish the course. Of course, to take notes you will require a pen and paper or a laptop/tablet. Even after 20 years of teaching, I'm still amazed at the number of students who turn up to lectures and tutorials without a pen or paper.

Review and write up your notes. This will fix the key learning points in your memory, enable you to answer any questions raised in the recap session at the start of the next lecture and help you contextualise the new material being covered.

Complete all pre-sessional reading you are set. Don't leave it to the last minute. Always take notes as you read. You want to be an active, not passive reader (see 5.8). Highlight anything you find interesting, don't understand or strongly agree or disagree with. Raise these issues at a suitable point during the session.

Complete any pre-sessional tasks you are set. For example, visit the library and find where the education journals are and what's available electronically. If, like many, you managed to graduate without ever setting foot in a library, now is the time to rectify that failing.

Interact with tutors and fellow students. Even if you are shy or come from a culture where it is not the norm to interact with your tutor, you must force yourself to enter into the discussions that are so much a part of Masters-level study in the West. Don't be afraid to challenge your tutor's views or express your own opinion, even if it's unpopular. Tutors will often present a position on an issue which they don't actually hold. They do it to provoke an argument, e.g. 'The best thing that the coalition government has done is to smash the idea that education is all about learning and give greater emphasis to the need for good teaching'. However, you must always be prepared to defend what you say by reference to either writers or other data you have collected on the subject (see 4.2).

Meet all deadlines set – no excuses. Even if your tutor lets you off, a missed deadline means that you have fallen behind and you'll now have to spend time on old material while trying to master new work.

Use feedback to improve your performance. Read all feedback that you receive from your tutors and act upon it in your next assignment. If you don't understand something, talk to your tutor. It's been my sorry experience to find that many students never read the feedback they receive on an assignment and that only a small percentage of them, usually the better students, act on the advice given. How can any student expect to improve if they don't take steps to address the weaknesses that have been highlighted in their previous work? They'll just go on making the same mistakes assignment after assignment and continue to wonder why their marks never improve.

SPACE FOR YOUR NOTES

3.4 Time-management strategies

Key point: If you waste money you can always earn more. If you waste time it's gone forever.

There is no doubt that studying for a Masters is a time-consuming business. This applies as much to part-time as full-time students. You need to work to a timetable, especially in the early weeks of your studies, if you are to balance the competing demands of your course, work, reading, research, completing assignments and trying to maintain some sort of family and/or social life. It can get tough if you're not organised. But there are things that you can do to find those elusive extra few hours a week that make the difference between success and failure.

I suggest that you ditch the daily to-do lists that form part of so many time-management programmes. Instead use the timetable in Handout 3.1 at the end of the chapter to list:

- your long-term (one to two years) objectives;
- your medium-term objectives (one to three months or a term);
- your short-term objectives (to be completed within the next one to four weeks).

Break these objectives down into a series of tasks. Completion of each task will move you closer to achievement of your objective. So for example:

- Your long-term objective is to pass your Masters.
- Completion of assignments one and two in the first term (three months) is an important medium-term objective, as is completion of assignments three and four in term two.
- Enter the above information on your calendar and then consider what tasks you need to complete in the next week to help you move towards your medium- and long-term objectives? Record these on your calendar as daily/weekly tasks.

Too often people devise a timetable that accounts for every minute of every day, and then feel guilty when they fail to stick to it. You need to exercise a sort of tight/loose control over your activities. You need some structure but you also have to allow for some flexibility. Provided you're constantly moving towards your objectives, it doesn't matter greatly if you are blown off track for a day or two, provided you recover your bearings and press on. The problem with just relying on a weekly timetable is that it can become a strait jacket, where putting the hours in becomes more important than achieving your aims and objectives.

Your timetable can be kept manually or in Excel or Outlook.

 Hint: Always timetable some time for family, friends, relaxation, hobbies and plain vegging out on the settee in front of the TV or games console. Sometimes when the pressure really starts to kick in the best thing you can do is take a day off and read a novel. But don't do it too often.

Every Sunday sit down and work out what you need to do in the week ahead to help you achieve your medium- and long-term objectives. This might be to attend the sessions at uni, read articles one, two and four, write 2,000 words of your draft assignment and send out your research **questionnaire**. Now the important thing to remember is that your aim is to complete the tasks and not spend a specified number of hours doing each task.

Having identified your tasks, prepare a timetable for the week ahead. Start by selecting one day on which you will do no work. This day doesn't have to be the same each week. Keep it flexible to accommodate those sudden changes in plan. This is important – you need one day a week to do the things that you want to do. To sleep, watch a film, or spend quality time with your partner, family or friends. On all the other days fill in the hours that are occupied by sleeping, eating and attending work or university. What is left is the time available for study, socialising and other activities that are so much a part of university life but which we are not going to go into details about!

Remember: From any period of study it is the quality of outcomes achieved that is important, not how long you spent looking at a book or screen with a glazed expression and thoughts a million miles away.

3.5 Time-saving hints

Key point: There are hundreds of ways to save time. Listed below are seven; use them as a prompt to identify others which you can use in your unique circumstances.

Study while you travel. If you find yourself living some distance from the university, use each journey as an opportunity to do some reading. For example, if you are travelling 45 minutes on the bus or train, that's an hour and a half reading per visit, or approximately 18,000 words (200 words per minute × 90) (see 5.8 and 5.9).

Learn to say no. Prioritise your activities and guard your time against time thieves. You don't allow people, even friends and family, to steal your money or property. Yet we are often happy for people to steal our time, involving us in activities that might be important to them but of no value to us. And unlike property or money, you can never recover time. Therefore, guard your time. It's the most precious commodity you have – and one day it will run out and you won't be able to negotiate an extension as you slide into the big sleep.

Learn to prioritise work. Your priorities are those jobs that move you closer to achieving your aim, i.e. successful completion of your Masters. Don't allow other people's priorities and crises, or your own wandering mind, to derail you. You have to be selfish and disciplined! That said, there will be times when your studies should rightly take second place to other important activities, like maintaining good relationships with family and close friends. It's very easy for you to forget that your family, partner and friends are not as excited as you are about your studies. Indeed, friends and family can quickly feel excluded from your new life. This can place a strain on the best of relationships. Don't let this happen to you. So build in some time every day for the people who are important to you.

Back up your files regularly. Keep a copy of all files on a memory stick, or other device, at a location away from your computer or laptop. Don't be like the third-year Ph.D. student who had every piece of work she had done for her Ph.D. on a single laptop with no backups! When it was stolen she was reduced to pinning up posters on trees around the university offering £1,000 for the return of her computer, no questions asked.

Learn to read faster. It's a sad fact that once we have been taught to read we never receive another reading lesson again. Yet by mastering just a few easy-to-learn techniques anyone can increase their reading speed by up to 100 per cent, while maintaining the same level of comprehension, in just a few weeks. The average reading speed is around 225–250 words per minute. Think how much time you could save if you increased that to even 350 words per minute (see 5.9).

Combine work and studies whenever possible. This strategy is particularly useful for employed part-time students. Think about basing all your assignments on an issue that is causing your school or organisation a problem. For example, if your school or college is keen to improve student performance, base your MA assignment on this issue. Then approach management and request permission to carry out research into the problem during the school day. They are unlikely to turn you down, and suddenly you find yourself collecting data and writing up research notes during the school day.

Study at work. If you work full-time, is there an opportunity during your lunch break or after work to do some studying. If you can find even half an hour a day this adds up to a useful 2.5 hours extra study time per week. Working after work may also have the added benefit of helping you to avoid the rush hour and so reduce travelling time.

 Remember: Avoid time-stealing vampires. They suck the life out of you.

SPACE FOR YOUR NOTES

3.6 Finding a time and place to study

As with the hints on how to save time, use the following as a starting point to draw up your own list of requirements. What those requirements are will vary. One student from Hong Kong told me that one of the happiest days of his life growing up was when his mother and father gave him the space under the kitchen table as his own. This was a rare luxury for a working-class child in the chronically over crowded island of Hong Kong – one which he used as his study space and which helped him fulfil his ambition of attending university.

 Remember: Many great people have studied in appalling conditions. That doesn't mean that you should do the same.

Identify if you are a lark or an owl. Larks are those annoying people who jump out of bed in the morning with a smile on their face ready to batter the world into submission with a barrage of smiles and positivity. I HATE THEM! How can anyone be cheery before 2 p.m.? Owls stumble out of bed, grunt through the morning and start to come alive about 2 in the afternoon. By 8 p.m. they are just hitting their stride. These are civilised people – just like me.

But seriously, knowing if you are a lark or an owl is important. If you're an owl it's a waste of time trying to get some quality study done first thing in the morning. Your body and mind will just not want to know. Knowing this is valuable information because it can help you to plan the most effective times for your study. Do the boring bits that have to be done early in the day – administration, photocopying and arranging meetings. And save the creative parts until later, when your mind is ready to do good quality work. If you are a lark, do your quality work in the morning and the other stuff later in the day.

Work 9 to 5. However, being an owl is not an excuse to stay in bed. As an autonomous learner you should look on your studies as a job and work normal office hours. Regardless of how many hours of lectures you have, arrive at the university at 9 a.m., and if there are no lectures/tutorials, go and work in the library. If your lectures finish early go to the library and study until 5 p.m.

We are creatures of habit. So make study a habit. You will be amazed at how much you can get done if you employ the 9-to-5 approach. And the beauty of it is you have far less work to do at home. It might be hard at first, but it gets easier. A bit of self-discipline is essential to the establishment of good study habits. And the temptations that every university has on offer will still be waiting for you when you have finished, with the added advantage that you won't be one of those students who have to leave the bar at 10 p.m. to prepare for the next morning's lecture.

Of course this 9-to-5 approach can't be applied to part-time students. But you might use a variation of it. Attendance patterns for part-time students vary widely between universities and courses. But at the very most you will be required to attend the university two nights a week. Pick one or two other evenings in the week that you will devote to study. If possible spend one of these evenings at the university.

Why am I so keen that you study at the university, you may ask? Well, it's a case of belonging. The more you attend the university, the more you will feel as if you belong. Not only that, you will quickly come to associate attendance with study.

Key point: Make study a routine habit.

A place of your own. When I started my doctorate I knew that I would be spending a lot of time in my study (a posh description for the box room at the top of the stairs with the boiler gurgling away next to it). So I went out and treated myself to a very posh second-hand wood-and-leather swivel chair. That chair has helped me write one Doctoral thesis and a few books. It was money well spent. Like the best Pavlovian response, whenever I sit in the chair I know that I must start typing.

At a bare minimum you need to identify a room, or part of a room, with a table and comfortable chair, which is quiet, has good lighting and ventilation, and is warm but not stuffy. This is your domain. When you are in it you are working and you don't want to be disturbed. Make that clear to family and friends and repel all those who want to steal your time. It may be hard and you may feel as if you are being selfish. You're not. You are marking out your time (see 3.4).

Remember: Find some place that you associate with study and use its familiarity to act as a trigger for study.

Attention span. Research suggests that our span of attention is about 45 minutes to an hour maximum. When studying we start off with a low level of attention. This gradually builds to a peak, which we maintain for a relatively short period of time before it starts to decline. While it will vary from person to person in a 45-minute session, our most productive period will be somewhere between the 8th and 37th minutes.

Regular breaks help you to reset your concentration. So after 45 minutes take a break. But restrict your time out to just a few minutes. Otherwise you run the risk of becoming distracted. After three 45-minute sessions take a longer break – between 30 and 40 minutes.

If possible vary your activities over the three sessions. For example, if you need to write an essay, write for 45 minutes. Then read for 45 minutes and then return to writing, or do some analysis for the final 45-minute session. When you return to your studies after your 30- to 40-minute break, repeat the cycle.

The success of this approach can be gauged from how well you are meeting your objectives for the week. Therefore, when drafting your timetable for the forthcoming week monitor your progress against objectives set for the previous week (see 3.4). That way you can check that you achieved all your objectives for the previous week and compensate for any shortfalls by increasing your workload the following week. If you've achieved more than planned in the previous week, give yourself a pat on the back and decide if you want to reduce your workload for the following week or if you want to work as normal and stay ahead of your objectives.

3.7 Where to find help and support

Although this chapter stresses that you must become an autonomous learner, you are not alone. The university wants you to succeed and will have its own unique support system. This will include, but may not be limited to, the following five sources of support:

- tutor/supervisor;
- personal development tutor (PDT);
- student services;
- student academic support;
- fellow students.

Who you speak to will depend on the nature of the problem and your personal relationship with staff and tutors. Full details of the support available to you will be outlined in the student handbook.

 Remember: Never be afraid to ask for help or advice. There will always be someone who can help you.

3.8 Conclusion

You may be familiar with many of the issues discussed in this chapter. But what's important is not familiarity with the ideas but whether you built them into your study habits. If not, what's the point of knowing them?

Do yourself a favour. Quickly review the contents of this chapter and identify which ideas you will put into effect when you start your Masters. With speed reading you could start tomorrow! For any ideas you reject ask yourself 'Why have I rejected this idea? Do I need to rethink my position?'

 Remember: Deposit tuppence worth of effort in your Masters account and you'll only get 2 pence worth of benefits back. Deposit everything you've got and you'll be able to draw on the account for the rest of your life.

SPACE FOR YOUR NOTES

Further reading

McGrath, J. and Coles, A. (2016) How to make time and space for your studies, in McGrath, J. and Coles, A. *Your Teacher Training Companion* (2nd ed.). Abingdon: Routledge.
Wilkinson, D. (2005) *The Essential Guide to Postgraduate Study*. London: SAGE.

HANDOUT 3.1   Time-management calendar

Study timetable week starting:

Annual/course objectives:	Termly objectives:
(1)	(1)
(2)	(2)
(3)	(3)

Weekly tasks:

(1)

(2)

(3)

Time	Sunday	Monday	Tuesday	Wednesday	Thursday	Friday	Saturday
09:00							
10:00							
11:00							
12:00							
13:00							
14:00							
15:00							
16:00							
17:00							
18:00							
19:00							
20:00							
21:00							
22:00							
Notes:							

4   Writing at Masters level

Aim of chapter: To provide you with the knowledge, skills and strategies required to communicate in clear, concise and unambiguous English at Masters level.

Chapter overview: This chapter explores writing at Masters level and concludes that good writers are able to explain complex ideas in clear, simple and unambiguous English. Advice is given on how this can be achieved by any student and it's suggested that all writers should follow the ABCs of good writing, i.e. accuracy, brevity and clarity. The need to support all claims made by reference to either literature or data is also emphasised.

4.1 Introduction

 Key point: Your aim when writing at Masters level is to express complex ideas as clearly as you can.

This is not a chapter on academic writing skills. If that's what you are looking for I suggest that you read Stephen Bailey's excellent book *Academic Writing: A Handbook for International Students*. Instead, this chapter assumes that you possess reasonable academic writing skills and sets out to show how to write successfully at Masters level.

No two people write in the same way. Some writers won't type a word until they are confident that it is the exact word they want to use. John Steinbeck took this approach and it meant that at the end of the day he would have 1,500 words ready for publication, of which he might change four words during editing. The majority of writers aren't like that. Most work using the multiple draft method. Jeffrey Archer, never before knowingly compared to John Steinbeck, stated that on some of his books he'd gone through 37-plus drafts.

The point is, you will have your own unique way of writing, which will develop as a result of your Masters studies, and it can be anything you like. Your aim is to present to your tutor a great assignment at the end of the process. How you get there is unimportant. It's the final product that counts. But I don't suggest that you try Raymond Chandler's approach. When he got stuck he'd go on a seven-day bender and produce a masterpiece at the end of it.

It's important that you know the audience you are writing for. On MA assignments your audience is your tutor/marker. Don't try to impress them by writing in a grandiose way (see 1.2), but at the same time don't write down to them. Academics hate to have their intelligence questioned/insulted.

If you follow the advice given below you will increase your mark on assignments by between 5 and 15 per cent. That is enough to turn a fail into a pass and a pass into a commendation. So read and, more importantly, apply the advice given.

4.2 Use data and/or literature to support any claims made

Warning: Never make unsubstantiated claims. Always back your claims up with literature or data.

We all like to tell people what we think – to expound our pet theories. Personally I've always believed that everyone is entitled to my opinion. But you need to save such diatribes for the pub. If you want to pass your Masters you must remember that your opinion counts for nothing.

All claims and statements, other than those that relate to common knowledge, must be supported by either literature or data. Common knowledge is any piece of information that is reasonable to assume your reader would know. For example, it's common knowledge in the UK that Margaret Thatcher was Prime Minister of the United Kingdom during the 1980s. However, it is not common knowledge that she based her economic policies on the work of Milton Friedman and Friedrich Hayek. If you wish to make that claim you'll need to support it with a suitable reference.

You must also avoid sweeping generalisations, such as 'Historically the Labour Party has been seen as the guardian of comprehensive education'. Labour's true relationship with comprehensive education, especially since 1997, is much more complex than this claim suggests. Similarly, to claim on the basis of six interviews that you have proved that the most effective teaching method is small group working smacks of delusions of originality. You must be circumspect and realistic when making any claims for your work.

Hint: It is better to under-claim in an assignment than over-claim. If it's a strong point your marker will recognise it as such and append a positive comment.

In order to write in a professional manner, avoid the use of adjectives and superlatives. Instead of writing 'I was amazed by the evidence that my six interviews produced . . . ', simply write 'I found . . . '. The reader will make up their own mind about how amazing your data is. Never make claims that your data cannot support. It's better to be conservative than to make grandiose claims which can be easily shot down by a critical tutor who has probably read the same thing a hundred times before.

Remember: KISS - Keep It Simple Stupid.

4.3 Use the past tense

This is a pet hate of mine, and the numbers of students using the future tense when writing their assignments are almost equal to the legions of hell. For example, statements such as the following regularly appear in students' work: 'I will interview six teachers' or 'I will use observations to *triangulate* data from my interviews'. When you write your assignment, you are reporting what you did, not what you are going to do. Therefore you must write in the past tense, i.e. 'I interviewed six teachers'.

4.4 Writing in the first or third person

'Should I write my assignments in the first or third person?' is often the first question that students ask when starting a Masters. Many psychologists, sociologists and those trained in the natural sciences argue that all academic work should be written in the third person. They adopt this approach because they seek to remain detached from the issues they are discussing, believing that this will improve their objectivity (see 6.3 and 6.11).

In education many of your assignments will be about your own professional practice. In such situations it seems plain daft to write 'The researcher observed the teacher using group and pair working', when the simple phrase 'I used pair and group working' is both clearer and reflects the reality of the teacher's involvement in what they are reporting/researching. However, what I think is not important. What your tutor wants is all that matters. Always follow the writing conventions laid down by your tutor/university. It is they who will determine if you pass or fail. So, if they demand that you write all assignments in the third person – give them what they want. Therefore, check what they want and deliver it.

 Remember: Once you have decided which approach to use, first or third person, do not switch between them in the course of your assignment. You must be consistent. Check which approach your tutor wants.

SPACE FOR YOUR NOTES

4.5 Accuracy and precision

The further you progress in your academic studies, the more important accuracy and precision will become. There can be no room for ambiguity or misunderstanding in what you write. You have to be precise. Just one significant error can undermine your tutor's confidence in your work, leading them to read the rest of your work with greater care as they look for the next big mistake. This can mean your submission is 'marked more strictly' than others – even if only subconsciously.

 Warning: Make one silly or serious mistake and your tutor will be looking out for the next. A case of, 'If they got that wrong what else have they messed up?'

Check and double-check all facts and claims that you've made. Reference all quotations correctly (see 5.10) and don't misinterpret what the writer said by editing a quote or piece of information to suit your argument. For example, many years ago a reviewer passing a London theatre was surprised to see on a hoarding the following quote attributed to him: 'The best play in London'. What he had actually written was 'This is not the best play in London'. By excluding just three words the theatre had changed the entire meaning of the review. Alas, students regularly 'try this on', thinking that their tutor may not have read the text referred to. But they wouldn't be your tutor if they were unaware of the author's stance on educational issues, would they?

There is an old saying: 'It's better to keep your mouth closed and have people think you are a fool, than to open it and remove all doubt' (Mark Twain, based on Proverbs 17:28). In writing, this translates to 'Never discuss an idea or theory unless you fully understand it'. Often we come to understand a complex concept by writing about it. Sometimes it's a struggle and we have to refer back to our books to make sure that our understanding is correct. That struggle should take place as you write drafts one, two and maybe three. If you are still struggling when it comes to your final draft, it's better to leave it out altogether than to demonstrate your lack of understanding and raise doubts in your tutor's mind as to your competence.

Similarly, if your work is badly structured (see 4.8), poorly written and littered with misspellings and grammatical errors, your tutor is likely to think 'This is sloppy and lazy, which probably means that their thinking and analysis is the same'. It's human nature. So use your spelling and grammar checkers but don't become over-reliant on them. The red wavy line will identify words which have been spelt incorrectly but it will not confirm that it is the right word. For example, *principle* and *principal*, and *there* and *their*. You have to check for such errors.

As for grammatical errors, when word processing look out for any sentences or words underlined with a green/blue wavy line. A green line does not mean go! It's an indicator that there is a possible error. What you have written may be a phase rather than a complete sentence or your punctuation is incorrect. Use the green line as a warning and play around with the sentence until such time as it disappears. The shorter your sentences, the less chance there is that you will make a grammatical error. Therefore, keep sentences under 20 words (see 4.7).

Remember: Tutors want to pass your assignment. Give them a reason to pass it by avoiding basic errors.

4.6 Brevity and meeting the required standards/criteria

Part of the challenge that you face at Masters level is answering the question set within the word limit. For assignments this is typically between 2,500 and 10,000 words. Dissertations are longer and can be anything from 10,000 to 25,000 words. Most universities insist that you do not exceed the word limit by more than 10 per cent. Write more and you can face a reduction of 10 per cent, the tutor only reading and marking up to the word limit plus 10 per cent or the work failing outright.

Hint: Digression is the enemy of brevity so don't digress: answer the question, the whole question and nothing but the question. Save interesting asides for discussion at coffee time.

The higher up the academic ladder you climb the more you will know about your subject – you'd be in trouble if you didn't. This is great, but it means that you have to make many more decisions about what to include in the body of your assignment, what to relegate to an appendix and what to exclude entirely. These decisions can be the difference between a bare pass and a good pass.

Any unnecessary or extraneous material must be cut from the work. But you have to ensure that what you have written meets the ***assessment criteria***. Read your assignment with a copy of the assessment criteria to hand and tick off each aspect of the criteria that you have covered as you come across it. This won't tell you how well you have addressed each criterion but will ensure that you cover all the requirements. When finished, look to see if there are any aspects of the criteria that you have not met and amend your assignment accordingly. Only then should you start to cut, cut and cut again. Sometimes you have to delete a paragraph that you spent hours perfecting, but if it's irrelevant it has to go. But don't start this process too soon (see 4.8).

Detailed information that you only refer briefly to once in your assignment can usually be relegated to an appendix and a summary of its main points included in the body of the text. For those readers who'd like to see the detail, refer them to the appropriate appendix. Information that is interesting but not essential, i.e. not directly relevant to your arguments, should be excluded entirely.

Hint: Most universities exclude material included in the list of references and appendices from the word count. This can help you meet the word limit without excluding material entirely from your assignment. Check what policy your university has.

In most assignments you will need to contextualise the issue you are discussing. For example, if you are exploring the advantages and disadvantages that free schools offer teachers, you'll need to outline the government's policy on this. Such information is essential if the reader is to understand the issues that you discuss. But keep it brief! If in doubt, discuss with your tutor the level of background information s/he expects.

Other strategies for achieving brevity are listed in section 4.7, because as well as saving words they help to improve the clarity of your work.

Remember: Even Mark Twain found it a challenge to express himself effectively in just a few words. Famously he wrote, 'I didn't have time to write a short letter, so I wrote a long one instead'. You have to learn to make every word count.

There are seldom any rules about being under the word limit. But check! It's risky to submit an assignment that is more than 10 per cent under the guideline figure. Why? Because, with fewer words it will be more difficult to answer the question to the standard required (see 2.6). This means that for a 5,000-word assignment you should aim for between 4,500 and 5,500 words. If you submit an assignment of 3,000 words, you'll need to be a writer of great skill to pass. A writer like Hemingway, who raised brevity and precision in writing to an art form, can get away with it. But then he was a Nobel laureate.

Warning: Check your university's policy on word limits. In a world where assignments are usually submitted online, it's very simple for your tutor to check the word count.

4.7 Clarity

Remember: When you write an assignment you are trying to communicate information that you have to your tutor. Therefore, eliminate anything that will get in the way.

When you write your assignment you are not writing a mystery story. You don't want to take the reader on a magical mystery tour. Instead, take them by the hand on a sightseeing tour from introduction to conclusion, pointing out all the important and interesting sights on the way. You achieve this by structuring your assignment in a clear and logical way (see Chapters 8 and 9) and following a few basic rules for writing effectively.

Warning: Don't spring any surprises on your tutor. If they are surprised, it means you haven't laid the groundwork for your claim/argument.

If you skipped section 1.2, which warned of the dangers of using big words and jargon, now is the time to read it as confusion often arises from the misuse of words.

The longer a sentence is the more chance you have of making a grammatical error which will distort or obscure its meaning. That's why *The Mirror* and *The Sun* newspapers, with most sentences under ten words long, make fewer grammatical errors than many of the broadsheets.

Many bestselling authors argue that a sentence should not exceed 12 words. But this is a challenge that even they don't always achieve. Therefore, aim for a maximum sentence length of 20 words. Each sentence should make one clear statement. The chances are that any sentence longer than 20 words will contain two or more sentences. The longest sentence that I've marked from a Masters student was 184 words. Needless to say, the sentence was neither clear nor unambiguous, and I can still remember how the will to live drained from me as I ploughed through it. (I retired shortly afterwards – disappointed that I'd never seen an example of the 200-plus word sentence!)

Paragraphs are important. Research has shown that the reader makes sense of what they have just read in the time it takes to move from one paragraph to the next. This implies that you should keep paragraphs as short as possible. But that would be incorrect and result in assignments that were little more than a list of bullet points.

A paragraph can be a sentence or a page long. What determines its length is that it discusses just one idea. For example, if you were talking about a particular teaching method, you might define/describe the method in paragraph one and then use paragraph two to discuss its strengths and three its weakness. Breaking down information into bite-sized chunks in this way makes it much easier for your tutor to understand what you are trying to say. What tutors don't want is a Joycean stream of consciousness that deals with multiple issues spread over several pages and without any paragraphs.

Warning: Your tutor can only give you a mark if they understand what you've written. Keep it simple and crystal clear.

In addition to expressing yourself in simple, clear terms you need to consider the tone of your writing. Ask yourself if it sounds arrogant, ineffectual and apologetic, or assertive and confident. You are supposed to be a master of the subject you are writing about, and how you write should reflect this. You need to write in a confident and assertive manner. For example: 'I found that . . . ' sounds a lot more confident than 'It's possible that my findings indicate that there is a chance that maybe . . . '.

To be able to write assertively you must have belief in what you have written, the facts presented and the interpretations you've placed on the data collected or literature used. Once you have this firm foundation you can critique your own work from a position of strength and identify ways in which you can improve your assignment (see 1.2).

Remember: Einstein said that 'Art is the expression of complex ideas in a simple form'. At Masters level you're not expected to produce a great work of art but you are trying to express complex ideas clearly.

4.8 The three stages of writing and checking what you've written

In every piece of writing there are three stages:

- creative
- organisational
- critical

In the creative stage you need to be uncritical and just get all your ideas down on paper. At this stage don't worry about the order, the spelling or the grammar. Just get it written. Only you will ever see these early drafts. Every writer's first and second drafts are an embarrassment, but without them they can never complete the job.

Once you have all the information you want on the paper, you can enter the organisational phase. This is where you rearrange what you have written. You move sections, paragraphs and sentences around until you are content that the presentation of information follows a logical sequence.

Only when you have structured your assignment and achieved a clear and logical narrative flow, with the right information in the right place, do you enter the critical phase. In the final critical phrase you should ask yourself the questions in Table 4.1.

Table 4.1 Assignment review questions

Questions	Yes	No
Have I addressed all the criteria at an appropriate level?		
Is what I have written factually correct?		
Have I supported all claims I've made with appropriate evidence from literature or data collected?		
Have I avoided making sweeping statements or generalisations?		
Is the work logically structured, both overall and within individual sections?		
Have I expressed my ideas clearly and unambiguously?		
Have I linked the paragraphs together so that one idea flows naturally into the next?		
Does the language I've used make it easy for the reader to understand and follow my arguments?		
Are there any words, sentences or paragraphs that I need to amend, extend, reduce or delete which would improve the strength and clarity of my arguments?		
Is the presentation of the work up to the standard required, e.g. all pages, tables and figures numbered, acceptable font used, etc.?		

Warning: Criticality is the enemy of creativity; it can paralyse you with fear. So don't become critical until you have completed the creative stage.

4.9 Use a critical friend

Once you have written and checked your assignment consider using a critical friend to independently check your work. They'll see good points that you can build on and errors that you've missed in your work. Don't ask either your partner or best friend to fill this role. Neither is likely to be as frank or critical as you require. They may also lack the understanding of what is required to produce a good assignment at Masters level. Besides, you can do without the arguments that will inevitably ensue. Instead, find someone on your course who you respect and get on with and negotiate with them a mutually beneficial relationship where they read and comment on your work and you do the same for them. Don't pick someone who is out to show how clever they are. Instead, select someone who is supportive and not afraid of giving or receiving criticism.

The basis of a good critical friend relationship is honesty and an understanding of what each person can expect. At a minimum, follow the advice given in Table 4.2.

Table 4.2   Essential rules for a successful critical friendship

> - To keep the relationship between you and your critical friend professional, draw up a **compact** at the start. This is an agreement which sets out the ground rules upon which you will both operate and what each of you can expect from the other person.
> - With each piece of work, give your friend a copy of the assessment criteria, which you'll find either in the course handbook or on the university's intranet, and ask them to check that you have addressed each element of the criteria fully.
> - Brief your friend on the issues that you want them to look out for specifically, e.g. poor or superficial analysis, clarity of English, padding, unsupported claims, contradictions in arguments, etc.
> - Agree on a timescale in which they will read your work and feed back to you. It's unreasonable to expect them to read and feed back to you within 24 hours simply because your deadline is looming. They have their own priorities.

If you don't want to use a critical friend consider using the university's AST. They can read and comment on the structure of your work, how logically organised the material is and your use of English. However, because the team are staffed by non-specialists, they can't comment on the content of your work or technical issues.

4.10 The buck stops with you

Whether you use a critical friend and/or the university's AST you remain responsible for what you submit. You can't pass the buck for errors and omission in your work. Therefore, I strongly recommend that when you have completed writing, editing and checking your assignment and run it past your critical friend/AST you put it in a drawer for a week and forget all about it. Then take it out for one final edit and polish prior to submission. You'll be amazed at what you find. Along with convoluted and poorly phrased sentences, missing words, under-developed ideas, ambiguities and quotes that aren't linked to anything, you will discover some really good writing, clever ideas and good examples of analysis and linking theory to practice which you can expand on further. But you will only spot these if you give yourself time to stand back from the work and review it with fresh eyes.

 Hint: As part of your final check read your assignments aloud before you submit them.

Provided you are a fluent English speaker, you are far more likely to hear an error than spot one on the page when reading silently. When reading aloud you are forced to slow down and instead of reading what you think should be there, you are more likely to read what you actually wrote. A second advantage is that you don't have to be a grammarian to spot errors. In many cases, the sound of the sentence will tell you it's wrong. Once the 'error' has been spotted, all you need do is play about with the sentence or paragraph until it 'sounds right'. In that respect it's similar to finding a way to make the green wavy line disappear on your Word document.

4.11 Conclusion

Too much academic writing is intended to impress the reader with the writer's knowledge and linguistic abilities. It should be about expressing complex ideas in clear and unambiguous prose which enlightens the reader rather than confuses them.

At Masters level some of the ideas you write about will be complex and difficult to explain/understand. It's your job to render them into a language that is understandable to your readers. Don't over-complicate things. Write as you would for an intelligent lay person. Define and explain all the terms and jargon that you use as you go along and you will end up with an assignment which clearly demonstrates your knowledge to the tutor – and that's what you are aiming for!

Further reading

Bailey, S. (2011) *Academic Writing: A Handbook for International Students* (3rd ed.). Abingdon: Routledge.
McGrath, J. and Coles, A. (2013) *Your Education Research Project Companion* (2nd ed.). Abingdon: Routledge, Ch. 2, 3 and 10.

HANDOUT 4.1   Guidelines on academic writing

- Good academic English communicates complex ideas in clear, simple terms that the reader can understand. It's not about jargon, big words or fancy phrasing.

- Use short sentences – fewer than 20 words.

- One issue = one paragraph.

- Keep to the word limit.

- Avoid being more than 10 per cent below the word limit.

- If acceptable to your marker, write in the first person.

- Always follow the ABCs of good writing: accuracy, brevity and clarity.

- Ensure that everything you write is factually correct and unambiguous.

- Avoid using unexplained jargon and/or abbreviations. If you have to use such terms, and sometimes you do, define them.

- Whenever possible, use a short word rather than a long one.

- Never use a word or phrase whose meaning you are unsure of.

- Never discuss an idea, theory or piece of data unless you understand it fully.

- Avoid adjectives and superlatives. They read like a poor novel.

- All claims/statements, other than those which relate to common knowledge, must be supported by either literature or data.

- Know the audience you are writing for. Do not write at such a level that they can't understand what you are saying, but don't insult their intelligence by writing down to them either.

5 Researching and writing a literature review

Aim of chapter: To enable you to find the literature you require and to write a critical literature review.

Chapter overview: This chapter provides advice on searching for literature both electronically and manually, keeping track of material read and lists the sources of literature that can be used in Masters-level work. It emphasises that it is not sufficient to report what writers have said but that all literature and data used must be subject to a process of critical evaluation. To assist busy students to read more widely, advice is given on both reading strategies they might adapt and how to increase their personal reading speed.

5.1 Introduction

Key point: If you don't know what other people have said about your subject how can you claim mastery of it?

A feature of studying at Masters level is that you are often required to write a stand-alone literature review. This is a requirement for most reports, research projects and any dissertation that you write at Masters level. You will be familiar with writing essays where you discuss what writers have said as part of the general discussion that forms the body of your work (see 9.4). However, many students find it difficult to discuss and evaluate their literature in one section and then use it in the findings to analyse, challenge, support and interpret the data they have collected. However, once you've done it a few times you'll find it relatively easy.

Warning: Avoid the situation where the first stand-alone literature review that you write is for your dissertation. Get some practice in before then.

It's only when you review the literature that you start to uncover the different perspectives on a topic and the arguments that rage among practitioners. This chapter will give you the information you need to find, critically evaluate and write up a literature review that can be properly described as a ***conceptual framework***. A conceptual framework is the body of theory that you are going to use to analyse and interpret your findings. For example, you could explore the growth of free schools and academies from either a communist/socialist perspective or a free market liberal/conservative perspective.

Many students worry that they may miss a vital article or book when searching for literature. This is unlikely. If you read four or five relevant articles that are up to date, they will probably contain over 100 references between them. Any ***seminal work*** in your area is very likely to be in that extended list. You will quickly identify seminal works by (a) What other writers say about a particular book or article and (b) The frequency by which it's referenced by other writers.

5.2 Undertaking a literature search

Remember: There are as many ways to undertake a literature review as there are students. The important point is to find the way that suits you best.

There is no perfect way to do a literature search. Most students use a mixture of 'wandering around the library with purpose' and using the various electronic search engines that are available. What's important is searching with a clear purpose in mind. This 'clear purpose' enables you to recognise relevant material when you see it.

To identify your purpose, exam the title of your assignment and the **research questions** that you are trying to answer (see 8.2). It is quiet common at Masters level for students to be asked to identify their own title/research questions and agree upon them with their tutor/ supervisor. This is part of becoming an autonomous learner (see 3.2) and is something that many students struggle with initially. Don't be in a rush to identify your topic, as the longer you spend studying a module the more ideas for potential assignments will arise.

5.3 Searching for literature manually

Once you are clear about the **research focus** (see 8.2) of your assignment you will be able to identify and record some of the keywords (terms) associated with the topic. You'll use these later as part of your electronic search. Unfortunately, at the start of your study you can't be certain that you know all the relevant keywords, hence the value of browsing the library shelves before engaging in any electronic search.

First, find the education journals in the library. The titles of some useful journals will be listed in the recommended reading for your module. But it's worth looking for more and not rely on being spoon-fed by your tutor. There won't be that many of them. Look at the table of contents in each journal over the last two or three issues and decide if it deals with the type of topics you are interested in. If it does, make a note of the journal's title. Even in a well-stocked library it will only take you a couple of hours to review all the education journals.

Once you've identified the most relevant journals, go through the back issues for the last five years and identify any articles that appear of interest. Do this by reading the abstract at the start of each article and checking the list of keywords provided. If you go back five years you will very quickly identify any seminal books or journal articles that were published earlier because they will be constantly referenced by later writers. Having read the later articles, you can decide if you need to consult the original seminal works or rely on a later summary of the material. With the exception of seminal works, anything older than five years runs the risk of being out of date.

You can also use your recommended reading list as the starting point for your review of books in the library. Try as far as you can to choose books that appeal to you rather than slavishly select every book of the reading list. If you like a book, there is a much better chance that you will read it than if you select a book you dislike simply because it was recommended.

If you use a seminal work extensively in your work, you should read it in the original and not rely on what other people have said about it. The writers you are relying on may not have read it in the original either and, like Chinese whispers, the original meaning can become twisted in the retelling. For example, many educationalists apply Abraham Maslow's hierarchy of needs to learners in a classroom without understanding the basis of the theory. Maslow's original work was based on white, Anglo-Saxon, protestant males who were mid-level executives in 1950s America. It was about how they sought to achieve self-actualisation over their careers/lives and not the course of a single lesson. Personally, I find it impossible to believe that anyone could achieve self-actualisation during a lesson on health and safety, no matter how good the teacher/lecturer/course was.

 Warning: If a seminal work or article is used extensively in your assignment you need to read it in the original and not rely on others to tell you what it says.

Some people find one really good up-to-date article or book and then use the list of references provided to trace other relevant books and articles. Unfortunately, writers very often reference other writers who agree with their views and arguments. This can result in biased articles which skew arguments in a particular direction. Never rely entirely on one major source. You may think that such **bias** would be picked up before publication. But just as different newspapers support a particular political party or policy, journals can have allegiances to particular academic tribes or ideologies. Even reputable academic book publishers are more concerned with sales than maintaining an unbiased balance, and as we know controversy sells books.

Once you have read a few articles in different journals you will start to see what the different editorial policies are. But don't worry too much about this. Markers are usually delighted to find that a student has accessed journal articles. Too many students rely almost entirely on a few textbooks.

 Remember: Read widely, doubt everything you read and constantly ask the question 'What evidence does the writer have for this statement?'

5.4 Searching for literature electronically

Having undertaken a manual library search, identified a number of articles and at least read their abstracts and list of keywords you will have a much better idea of the keywords that relate to your topic. Use this list for your electronic searches.

Use the **British Education Index (BEI)** as the basis of your electronic search. Find the electronic resources button on the university's library page, look for BEI and a search page will open up. Enter your keywords on the search page and press Find and you'll get back a list of publications. Some returns will only display the abstract for a publication but many will contain a full text version of the publication – depending on which journals your university subscribes to. There are other indexes you could search but I suggest you concentrate on the BEI and its American cousin **Education Resources Information Center (ERIC)**. If you have trouble finding either ask the librarian for help.

Hint: Use different terms and combinations of terms to maximise the number of relevant hits you get.

You should also use Google Scholar because it focuses on academic and **peer-reviewed** sources and includes abstracts. Peer review is the process whereby a paper is reviewed by experts in the field prior to its publication. They can accept or reject the work for publication or ask for changes to be made to it before it is published.

A major advantage of Google Scholar is that articles are ranked by the number of citations each has attracted, with the most popular articles listed first. You can even click on 'Cited by' and see a list of all the documents that have cited the source. Effectively, this means that anyone who has cited the entry is writing in a similar area, and you might want to check out their work as it will be more up to date.

Warning: Don't ever approach your tutor and say that you couldn't find anything on your area of interest. With just a few clicks of the mouse they will reveal the mountain of material that you couldn't find. Which is very embarrassing.

SPACE FOR YOUR NOTES

5.5 Keeping a record of what you've read

Record the full reference (see 5.10) of any article or book that your manual or electronic search throws up and which you intend to use. Make a brief summary of its contents and jot down keywords. You should aim to get all the information on one side of a 6 × 4 index card or half a page on a Word document.

Remember: You don't need to summarise the whole article or book. You just need to summarise what is relevant to your studies. So keep referring back to the focus of your assignment and your research questions.

This process of continual reference back to your research questions will help you stay focused on the issues that are relevant and not be side-tracked by interesting but extraneous factors. It will also help you to break down your focus into its component parts. Often your questions will be concerned with two or more ideas. For example, 'How can the use of learning styles theory help improve children's behaviour in the classroom?' Can you see that before you can answer that question you need to discuss what is meant by learning styles and a range of theories about the causes of poor behaviour in the classroom?

5.6 What counts as literature?

A wide range of material can be used as literature. But some sources have greater academic credibility than others. The list in Table 5.1 is ranked according to its **_provenance_**, with the academically respected sources such as journals and seminal books near the top and the less-respectable stuff at the bottom – such as TV, radio and the Internet. Thus literature with the best provenance are articles that have been peer reviewed and published in academic journals of international renown, followed by journals with a national reputation. Books appear below these because they have not been peer reviewed although some chapters may have been reviewed by the publisher's advisors prior to publication.

Table 5.1   Sources of academic literature in descending order of academic credibility

- Peer-reviewed journals with an international reputation.
- Peer-reviewed journals with a national reputation.
- Seminal books by authors with a high academic reputation.
- Books by authors with a high academic reputation.
- Acts of Parliament, White Papers, Green Papers, government reports, reports and papers from local government and quasi non-governmental organisations (quangos), e.g. the Office for Standards in Education (Ofsted). **Note that these reports, while important, are not unbiased.**
- **_Professional journals_**, including publications by professional bodies, trade unions and employer organisations.
- Quality press publications such as the *Times Educational Supplement*, *Times Higher Education*, *The Economist* and *The Spectator*.
- The broadsheet newspapers, including *The Times*, *The Guardian*, *The Independent* and *The Telegraph*.
- Quality TV and radio documentaries and Teachers TV.
- You will note that no mention has been made of the Internet. This is because web sites range in academic quality from the highly respectable and influential to absolute dross. When using web sites it is imperative that you critically evaluate the provenance of the site. For example, who funds and runs the site, what is its editorial policy and how often is material updated.

It is not necessary that you use literature from every source listed above. But it is important that you use a range of literature, including as a minimum requirement material from:

- journal articles;
- books;
- respected web sites.

What you are aiming for is a balanced selection of articles, books, reports and reputable web sites. Increasingly, examiners expect to see several web addresses amongst your list of references.

Often students ask how many references they need for an assignment. That's the same as asking how long is a piece of spaghetti (I've always found that it's just long enough to stain my shirt). As a general rule, I would argue that it's better to use fewer references and use them well than to triple the number you have and barely refer to 80 per cent of them in your assignment. Whichever approach you adopt, it's inevitable that for every reference you include you will have to exclude two or three others that you have read and sweated over.

Remember: At Masters level what you leave out is as important as what you include. Make the wrong decision and you can be in trouble.

SPACE FOR YOUR NOTES

5.7 Critical evaluation

Remember: Critical evaluation is essential at Masters level.

Don't trust anything you read. Instead, try to critically evaluate everything you read. The quickest and easiest way to do this is to find another writer in the same field who holds a different viewpoint. For example, if you're writing about the value of learning styles, I would expect you to look at Frank Coffield's seminal 2004 report, *Learning styles and pedagogy in post-16 learning*. In it he calls into question the validity of many, if not most, learning style theories and demonstrates how few of them are based on actual research.

It is rare to find two writers who disagree 100 per cent on an issue. More often you'll find that different writers will agree on 80 or 90 per cent of an issue. But it is the 10 or 20 per cent that they disagree about which you need to search out and highlight in your review, because this is where the detail of their arguments rests. Discussing the various shades of opinion that exist is what you should be addressing at Masters level.

To compare and contrast the work of writers is a challenge and can require a lot of words. Fortunately, you don't have to do it for every piece of work used. What you want is to demonstrate that you do not just accept what writers say, and imply that if only you had more space you would critically evaluate every piece of writing. Your marker knows that there are limits to how critical you can be in the space available. They just want evidence that you understand how important it is and that you can do it.

In addition to comparing and contrasting what writers say on a subject, you can also use any of the approaches listed in Table 5.2.

It won't be possible for you to submit the work of every writer you use to all the above checks. Instead, keep the list in mind and as you read an article look for signs that the writer may have breached one of the above guidelines. If you spot this, make a note of it and include a comment in your literature review.

To demonstrate clearly to the reader that you have tried to be critical, litter your literature review with such phrases as 'X agrees with Y on this issue because . . . ' but 'in contrast, Z takes the view that . . . ', or 'X argues against this view . . . ', 'This view is contested by Z' or 'This claim does not appear to be supported by any primary research'.

Remember: Quoting and summarising the writings of others is not a high-level academic activity. What marks out good work is critical evaluation. Without that you will only score in the 40s or low 50s.

Table 5.2   Ways to critically evaluate literature

- Consider the provenance of the work. Has the work been peer reviewed?
- Is the work supported by research data? How reliable is the data used?
- Is the work based on the person's personal experience? If so, how have they dealt with bias (see 6.11).
- Are the writer's arguments logical and reasonable?
- What are the weaknesses of the work?
- What literature or research data has been used to support the arguments put forward?
- Has the writer used the views of a range of authors to challenge the data they have collected and their interpretation of it?
- Have any claims for cause and effect been made? (It's notoriously difficult to prove cause and effect in the social sciences as many of the variables in play can't even be identified, let alone controlled.)
- Was the research approach adopted appropriate/adequate? How much reliance can you place on the findings?

5.8 Improving your reading strategies

Hint: Read widely. Even if you don't use everything you have read in your litera-ture review, it will be reflected in the quality of your thinking, which will shine through in your work and be reflected in the mark awarded.

When was the last time that you had a lesson on how to read? I've always thought it strange that once we have taught a child to read we never go back and tell them how they can improve their reading speed and comprehension. Yet today teachers and other profes-sionals are deluged with stuff they have to read. By registering on a Masters programme you are signing up to a mountain of reading! There is no escaping this reading if you want to achieve a good mark. However, by learning and applying a few 'tricks of the trade' you can improve your reading speed, without any reduction in your comprehension, by 50 per cent with very little effort.

To achieve an improvement in your reading speed you need to develop a range of time-saving reading strategies. The first is discrimination. Instead of reading in full every book or article that might be relevant, ask yourself 'Do I need to read, understand and remember the contents of this document or do I just need to know roughly what it says and where I can find it if I need to know more?' Asking this simple question can save you hours of reading in detail stuff that you may never use.

If you decide that you need to read something, decide what you want to get out of a source before you start. Refer to the focus of your research and research questions when drawing up this list. Then selectively read the parts of the document that are relevant to your needs. Use the abstract and subheadings in articles to identify the relevant parts of the arti-cle and perhaps start with the conclusion to see if the work is about what you think it is. With books, use the table of contents, chapter headings, summaries and, most important of all, the index to locate the key information that you need. Because your assignment is narrowly focused, only very rarely will you need to read a book from cover to cover.

Learn to skim read and not feel guilty about not reading every word. Try reading the first and last sentence of each paragraph. The first sentence will tell you what the paragraph is about and the last will often sum up the writer's conclusions on that issue.

Hint: If you are reading any report, check to see if it has an executive summary and read that first.

If you have a specific purpose in mind when you start to read, you'll be on the lookout for keywords and phrases, and when they appear they'll jump off the page at you. When that happens, slow down and read the paragraph or section in full.

Once you have identified important information, remember to highlight it. You can do this with a highlighter pen on hard copies of books (not library books – the library hit squad will have your guts for garters if you deface a book, and rightly so). Use different colours – that way you can colour-code different themes as they arise. You can also highlight electronic records and even copy selected quotes directly into a literature file. However, whenever you do this be very careful and use a different font colour so that you don't include someone else's work as your own. You don't want to be accused of plagiarism.

With the growth of the Internet, plagiarism has become a hot topic in universities. It has never been easier to find an article or essay on the Internet and pass it off as your own work. Plagiarism is the greatest academic crime and the way to avoid it is to be scrupulous in your referencing (see 5.10).

 Warning: If you can find an essay or report on the Internet to plagiarise, your tutor will also be able to find it! It's not worth the risk.

Try to read actively. This requires you to enter into a dialogue with the writer, e.g. do I agree with what the author says here? If so why? If not, why not? Or what evidence does the author have to say this? Not only does this improve your powers of critical evaluation, it helps you to stay engaged with what you are reading and helps you to remember and recall what you've read. Make a note of these 'musings' next to any highlighted section.

SPACE FOR YOUR NOTES

5.9 Improving your basic reading speed

To improve your actual reading speed you have to stop reading one word at a time and learn to read three, four or more words simultaneously. This can double your reading speed without decreasing your level of comprehension. Achieving it is easy, provided you are willing to practise what is suggested below.

Start by selecting a passage from a book and see how many words you can read in a minute while still understanding what the passage says. Get someone to time you for exactly one minute and count how many words you have read in that time. This is your baseline reading speed. The average person reads between 225 and 250 words per minute.

Once you have this baseline, try to get rid of ***sub-vocalisation***. When you learnt to read you read aloud. When you progressed to silent reading you continued to hear the sound of the word in your mind. This listening for the sound of the word is sub-vocalisation and it slows you down almost as much as if you had read the word aloud. Yet there is no need for it because your mind registered what the word meant long before you heard the sound.

Sub-vocalisation is a habit, and like most habits it is very difficult to break. What you need to do is force yourself to read so quickly that you don't have time to hear the word.

To achieve this soundless reading aim to read two or more words simultaneously. Again, because we learnt to read by pointing at single words we tend to continue reading one word at a time. This slows us down further because we have to move our head and/or eye to focus on each word. It is this mechanical movement of the head and the eyes and our sub-vocalisation that wastes time. We are all capable of seeing and comprehending four or five words simultaneously. But we persist in reading each word because we think we have to. If you don't believe me, consider how quickly you read instructions flashed up on computer games.

At first it will feel unnatural, but if you stick at it for six weeks you will have replaced an old habit with a new one and it will feel entirely natural. At first, try 'soundless speed' reading for 15 minutes a day for a few weeks, then slowly introduce it into your everyday reading.

Hint: To practise reading two, three or four words at a time, get a newspaper and, using a ruler, run the rule down a column while keeping your head still and your eyes focused on the centre of the column. You will be amazed at how much information your peripheral vision picks up when you try this. And because you are reading more than one word at a time, it will assist you in getting rid of sub-vocalisation.

Remember: At first, speed reading can feel alien as you are trying to change the habits of a lifetime. But keep at it and after about six to eight weeks it will become your new norm.

5.10 Referencing and plagiarism

Warning: Plagiarism is the cardinal sin of academia. A lecturer can survive all sorts of scandals but they never recover from a charge of plagiarism – nor do students.

Some overseas students find the West's obsession with referencing odd. They are used to assuming that their tutor knows the source of the information they are using and therefore a reference is not required. Perhaps because of the West's commitment to individualism it is necessary to acknowledge the work of specific individuals when their work is used. While I might agree that any discussion on referencing is about as exciting as watching two flies crawl up a window, it is vitally important that you learn and apply the referencing system used by your university.

Table 5.3 Why referencing is important

- It protects you against charges of plagiarism, i.e. passing off the work of others as your own. If such a charge is proved, you could be dismissed from the course.
- It allows the reader to follow up a reference that they wish to check and/or read more about.
- Poor referencing demonstrates a slap-dash approach to academic work and leads your tutor to think 'If they can't be bothered to get the referencing right, why should I rely on anything else they write?'

There are various systems of referencing, including:

- Modern Humanities Research Association (MHRA) referencing system;
- American Psychological Association (APA) referencing system;
- University of Chicago system;
- Harvard University system.

If I were to describe each system in detail, you'd be chewing your hand off with boredom, as discussing different referencing systems is about as interesting as talking to a tin of beans. However, referencing is important, therefore I leave it to you as an autonomous learner and Masters student to find out what system is in use in your faculty/university. The information you require will be in your student handbook or available from the library. It is also extremely likely that the student academic support team will run sessions on referencing and have useful handouts on the subject.

I accept that learning to reference material is tedious, but once you've mastered the skill it's surprisingly easy to use and you quickly find yourself critiquing writers who don't reference material correctly.

 Remember: There are minor variations within all referencing systems that are allowable. For example with the Harvard system the page number can be shown as p., P. or page. The important thing to remember is that you must be consistent. Use one style of referencing within your chosen system and apply it consistently.

5.11 Conclusion

Many Masters students find it difficult, and even embarrassing, to critically evaluate published writers. They are worried that they will make a fool of themselves and feel that they don't have the right to criticise the experts. But everyone has to start somewhere. If it's not at Masters level – when? Yes, you'll make mistakes at first and some of your criticisms will be weak and easily rebuffed. But you are learning. You are starting to join in with the academic debate. Which is exactly what you should be doing.

Another element of the academic debate that you must come to terms with is the need to be scrupulous in your referencing and avoid any hint of plagiarism. If you fail on either front you will undermine your academic career/reputation before it's even got off the ground.

SPACE FOR YOUR NOTES

Further reading

McGrath, J. and Coles, A. (2013) *Your Education Research Project Companion* (2nd ed.). Abingdon: Routledge.
McGrath, J. and Coles, A. (2016) *Your Teacher Training Companion* (2nd ed.). Abingdon: Routledge.
Ridley, D. (2012) *The Literature Review: A Step-by-Step Guide for Students*. London: SAGE.

HANDOUT 5.1   The literature review

The literature review

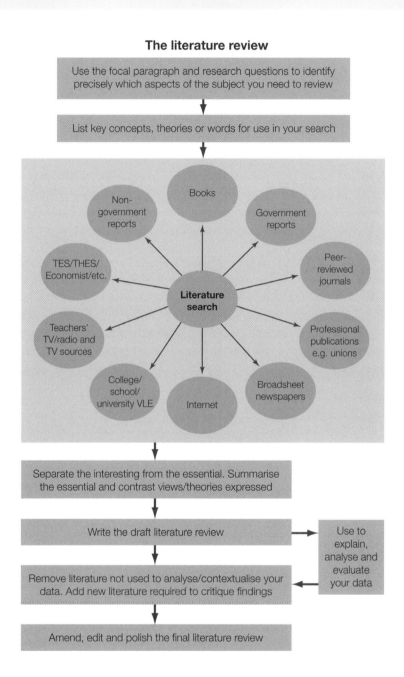

Use the focal paragraph and research questions to identify precisely which aspects of the subject you need to review

List key concepts, theories or words for use in your search

Books

Non-government reports

Government reports

TES/THES/Economist/etc.

Peer-reviewed journals

Literature search

Teachers' TV/radio and TV sources

Professional publications e.g. unions

College/school/university VLE

Internet

Broadsheet newspapers

Separate the interesting from the essential. Summarise the essential and contrast views/theories expressed

Write the draft literature review

Use to explain, analyse and evaluate your data

Remove literature not used to analyse/contextualise your data. Add new literature required to critique findings

Amend, edit and polish the final literature review

(McGrath, J. and Coles, A. (2013) *Your Education Research Project Companion* (2nd ed.). Abingdon: Routledge, p. 72.)

6 Your research methodology

> **Aim of chapter:** To introduce you to the language of research.
>
> **Chapter overview:** This chapter introduces the essential research terminology that all Masters students must be familiar with. Specifically it explains such concepts as a researcher's **ontological** and **epistemological** stance, what is meant by **interpretivist** and **quantitative** methodologies and three popular **research strategies** at Masters level, namely case studies, **action research** and **surveys**. It ends by explaining a range of key concepts/terms that all researchers must discuss in their final report or dissertation including: bias, **ethics**, **validity** and **reliability** and triangulation.

6.1 Introduction

 Key point: Primary and/or secondary research are an essential element of Masters-level study. The sooner you can familiarise yourself with the terminology used the easier it will be for you to make progress.

Some Masters-level students think that if they are to achieve the highest marks at Masters level, their research has to produce new and original work. Let's be absolutely clear about this. **You are not required to produce original work at Masters level; that is only required at Doctoral level.** Many students achieve very high marks by researching areas that numerous students and writers have tackled, such as classroom management, teaching styles, learning styles, use of information and communication technology (ICT) in the classroom, etc. It is the quality of your work and not its originality that will determine if you pass or fail. However, it's worth remembering that if you research your own setting or practice, your data and findings will be unique to that time and setting. So it's almost certain that a by-product of your research will be an element of unintended originality.

Warning: The aim of this chapter is to introduce you to the philosophical foundations upon which research methodology rests and the research strategies you can adopt when undertaking your research. It does not provide the depth or breadth of information that you will need to write a good research methodology section at Masters level.

This chapter will introduce you to the language of research and dispel some of the mystery that surrounds the process. It will also prepare you to read the research books with a better understanding.

The defining characteristic of study at Masters level is research. Every Masters course will require you to undertake either primary or secondary research. **Primary research** is where you collect and analyse data of your own. Secondary research is where you rely on the work of other researchers. This might be literature or findings from previous research that is in the public domain.

 Key point: Try and undertake some primary research during your Masters course. The skills learnt are both invaluable and transferable to numerous situations in life; from buying a new car to finding ways to improve your organisation's performance and improving your own professional practice.

6.2 A word on research terminology

 Warning: One of the odd things about research is that, for a process which demands precision and detail, there is precious little agreement on the definitions for many of the terms commonly used. What I have tried to do in this and the next chapter is to simplify the discussion and talk about the four levels of research:

- At the top level you have the broad philosophical and conceptual issues, such as 'what is the nature of research?' What is your ontological and epistemological stance? Is your research based on a *positivist* or *anti-positivist* philosophy (see 6.3)?
- The next level, methodological approaches, include *quantitative* or *qualitative* approaches to research. I describe these as methodological approaches. Basically the methodology is concerned with the overarching principles that underpin the research.
- Below the methodology sits what I call the 'research strategies', such as *experiments*, *case study*, action research and surveys. These strategies are used to organise and structure the research; to delineate the boundaries of the research and maintain control over the project. Other writers describe some of these approaches as methodological approaches (see Denscombe 2014).
- Finally, there are the research methods, which are the tools used to collect the data, such as *interviews* and questionnaires. These are discussed in Chapter 7.

6.3 The philosophy of research: your ontological and epistemological stance

 Warning: The material discussed in this section is difficult to understand. Don't worry if you can't understand it even after a couple of readings. At this stage you just need to know that these terms exist. Read the definition of each in the Glossary of Terms at the end of the book.

Key point: In your research methodology section, the first thing you have to discuss is your ontology. If you believe, as scientists do, that there is only one reality and it is the job of researchers to discover that reality, you would be described as a positivist. But if you believe that reality is at least partially constructed by each individual person, then you are an anti-positivist. Effectively, your ontology describes how you view the social world.

The positivist's viewpoint is easy to understand. But the anti-positivist's seems strange. How can there be multiple realities? Don't we all live in the same world? Let's look at the example of two Parisian residents. A woman's experience of living in Paris would be different from a man's. They may both travel to work on the Métro, do the same job and go out and socialise at the same venues, etc. But they will have different experiences and may react very differently to similar experiences. In the end, each will view Paris through the lens of their own unique experiences, and this becomes their reality.

Therefore, when we talk of different realities we aren't talking about diametrically opposed views of reality. It's just that people perceive certain issues and events differently from others and the sum of these differences creates 'their reality'.

 Key point: Epistemology is concerned with knowledge and what constitutes knowledge. If you are a positivist, you believe in the scientific approach to the discovery and verification of knowledge. For positivists, knowledge has to be testable, and the results obtained from a single experiment must be repeatable for the findings to be valid. Therefore, you'd only be interested in data that can be transmitted in tangible form, such as facts and figures.

 Key point: If you are an anti-positivist you will accept people's opinions, views, attitudes and beliefs as valid knowledge.

Much of the research that is undertaken in education is concerned with people's feelings, attitudes and beliefs and will be anti-positivist in nature, i.e. concerned with what people see as their reality. Many positivist researchers, and politicians, are critical of this form of research and argue that it is not underpinned by scientific rigour. However, this actually says more about their ontological beliefs than the value of the research they are criticising.

This dispute has given rise to what is known as the **paradigm** wars. A paradigm is a way of thinking and organising ideas into a coherent pattern. The anti-positivists have developed the interpretivist paradigm. Within this there are a number of different approaches that researchers can adopt. These include qualitative, **phenomenological**, **grounded theory** and **ethnographic** approaches to research. Although they are all different they share certain characteristics, for example, they all believe that individuals have at least some control over their lives, and they are **ideographic** in that they focus on the lived experiences of individuals.

As an interpretivist you recognise that educationalists work in a range of 'realities' and one hypothesis can't explain all situations. Therefore, you would be interested in developing a range of hypotheses to explain people's different realities rather than proving a single hypothesis.

In contrast, positivists believe that individuals are controlled to a considerable extent by social structures, relations and rules. In other words, people live in a **deterministic** world. It follows, therefore, that they think it is necessary to look at large groups of people, not individuals, if they are to discover the single reality that is the social world. They use quantitative and scientific approaches to research, including experiments.

If you are a **realist**, you will almost certainly employ a scientific approach to research. This means that you will establish a **hypothesis** and then seek, through experiment and **observation**, to confirm or refute the hypothesis.

SPACE FOR YOUR NOTES

6.4 Quantitative and qualitative approaches to research

Hint: Many Masters students adopt either a quantitative (positivist/scientific) approach or qualitative (anti-positivist/interpretivist) methodology, and it is these that I suggest you consider as your first choices.

Remember: Quantitative and qualitative methodologies are often represented as opposing paradigms, with qualitative research exploring people's attitudes, beliefs, feelings and perceptions, and quantitative research concerned with numbers, quantities and observable facts.

This oppositional view isn't very helpful. The truth is most research contains elements of both approaches. Every Masters student should read Chapter 3 in Richard Pring's (2003) excellent book which discusses the false dualism of education research, in which he argues against this idea. However, although there are several ways to show the differences between these approaches the clearest way for me to explain them is to pose them as a series of opposites.

Cohen et al. (2011) suggest that very often the purpose of quantitative research is to test a theory or verify a claim. This may involve carrying out controlled experiments, counting or measuring some phenomena such as exam results, or collecting data from statistical records, detailed observations, questionnaires or experiments. The idea is to be as objective as possible. To achieve this, the researcher tries to minimise any effect that their own beliefs, values and opinions might have on the data. They remain detached from the research participants and the data they collect from them. The nature of the data they're interested in is hard, impersonal and factual, and they seek to generalise their findings across time and beyond the location in which they collect the data. A key feature of such research is the need to identify, control and account for all the **variables** that are at play. Data can be collected from published statistics, observations, questionnaires, interviews and experiments.

Conversely the purpose of qualitative research is to generate theories, not to verify them. It is concerned with discovery rather than proof, and the researcher attempts to collect data without interfering with the normal flow of life, i.e. they don't seek to control the variables at play in the situation. Rather, they seek to identify what variables are in play. Data can be collected using observations, interviews, questionnaires and focus groups, and will describe attitudes, beliefs and feelings. However, the nature of the data means it isn't possible to accurately measure the phenomena under review. The values of the researcher and the relationship they have with the respondents also affect how the data are interpreted. Effectively, the researcher uses their own knowledge, experience and understanding to make sense of it, and in doing so create their own version of the data (Denscombe 2014).

While your research is likely to be qualitative in nature, it is possible to fine-tune it and include an element of quantitative research. For example, many qualitative researchers use **Likert**-style questions (see 7.6) and ask their respondents to say, on a scale of one to five, how they feel about a series of questions. This produces numbers which you can manipulate and report using quantitative methods. However, you should realise that what you are doing is reporting qualitative data in a quantitative form, because the rating given by the teachers for various statements is effectively just a descriptor of their qualitative feelings and perceptions. In addition, whenever you assess people's opinions, there will always be variation in how they interpret and understand the question you've asked. This is why caution is needed when analysing semi-quantitative data such as this. Never construct your entire argument based on one source of data.

6.5 Other interpretivist approaches to research

In 6.3 I referred to a range of research approaches that interpretivists have developed. I would recommend that you adopt a qualitative approach whenever possible. However, for the sake of completeness I have outlined some of the less used, but interesting, approaches that are available to you and the reasons why they are rarely used at Masters level. These include ethnographic, phenomenological and grounded theory approaches.

Ethnographic studies. The word 'ethnography' comes from the Greek *ethnos*, meaning *people*, and *graphein*, meaning *to write*. So it's not surprising that ethnographic research refers to specific groups of people, their beliefs and behaviours. The groups could be defined or bounded by some common criterion such as religion or culture. The aim of your field work would be to gather enough data to present a highly detailed picture of the group being studied. You'd be interested in how the group viewed the world, the meanings that they gave to events and their customs, rituals and beliefs.

 Warning: To achieve the level of detail required you would have to immerse yourself in the lived lives of these people and you would end up with a vast amount of data – far more than you could possibly fit into a Masters project or dissertation. So I would recommend that you avoid doing an ethnographic study at Masters level – save it for your Ph.D.

If you think that ethnographies are only relevant to some lost tribe in the Amazon you'd be wrong. Great studies have been done on football hooligans, motorcycle gangs and, perhaps most famously in British education, Willis's study of a group of school leavers in *Learning to Labour* (1981).

Phenomenological studies explore how people interpret and react to the events and experiences (the phenomena) they encounter as they travel through life, and how these help the person to build up their own view of reality. As such, phenomenology is as much a branch of philosophy as it is research. Many of its followers think that the whole of human knowledge can be explained in this way.

 Warning: Again, I would not recommend it for Masters-level work because the phenomenologist's task is to present their data in a way that is faithful to the original (Denscombe 2014). This requires a considerable amount of description and detail, which takes up a great deal of space and leaves little room for analysis and evaluation, which are usually criteria that you have to meet.

The above is not a criticism of the phenomenological approach, rather a suggestion that it's more appropriate to Doctoral level work, where you have up to 80,000 words to play with.

Grounded theory studies are particularly interesting, as the approach is almost a complete reverse of the traditional 'scientific' method. In grounded theory research data are first collected and then categories identified. After a process of constant refinement and integration, the resulting categories are then used to formulate theory. Traditionally, a literature review isn't carried out beforehand, as this may influence the coding process and therefore the theory generated.

This is a fascinating approach but beware. The original model from Glaser and Strauss (1967) suggests that you should go through a ten-stage process. Their process is very stringent and time-consuming, and stage four (saturate categories) requires the researcher to continue collecting data from different participants until no further new categories of information are found. Only at that point have you achieved saturation point and can start to build your theory. This represents an open-ended commitment to the collection of data; a commitment which no student with a deadline should enter into, as you wouldn't be able to predict how many interviews, observations or whatever you had to carry out in advance. The approach was revised by Strauss and Corbin (1990) but it still contains seven stages that you have to follow.

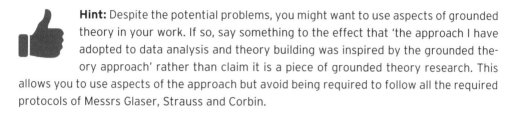

Hint: Despite the potential problems, you might want to use aspects of grounded theory in your work. If so, say something to the effect that 'the approach I have adopted to data analysis and theory building was inspired by the grounded theory approach' rather than claim it is a piece of grounded theory research. This allows you to use aspects of the approach but avoid being required to follow all the required protocols of Messrs Glaser, Strauss and Corbin.

SPACE FOR YOUR NOTES

6.6 Research strategies

There are a range of research strategies available to the researcher at Masters level and it's important to choose the most appropriate one for your research. The vast majority of small-scale educational research projects or dissertations are covered by *case studies*, action research and surveys. These are conceptually straightforward, easy to grasp and flexible enough to address a range of research questions. It's also the case that action research has become the method of choice to support professional development in professions such as teaching, nursing and social work. Less popular are experiments and **quasi-experiments** which tend to be used by those who hold an objectivist ontology.

Hint: Many Masters students choose to present their research in the form of a case study. That's fine. However, in the majority of cases, one data collection method has usually generated the vast bulk of the data reported (see 6.9). In such cases the work should be presented as a survey.

Surveys are less complex than case studies, easier to describe and defend and take up less room to explain than a case study. Therefore, as part of my belief in Keep It Simple Stupid I would recommend that you stick with a survey, if possible.

Table 6.1   Research strategies available to subjectivist and objectivist researchers

Anti-positivist Subjectivist strategies	Positivist Objectivist strategies
Case study	Case study
Surveys	Surveys
Action research	Not applicable
Possibly quasi-experiments	Experiments and quasi-experiments

6.7 Case studies

Case studies are a particularly popular strategy with Masters students. A case study is the exploration of a bounded ***instance*** using multiple data collection methods which results in a highly detailed picture of the person, place or thing under examination.

The term 'bounded' is particularly important in this definition. As a sole researcher you have to find some way to limit the size of your enquiry. For example, as an education researcher, one of your first decisions will be what you are going to 'look at' – is it one person, one class, one year group, both sexes, just one sex, etc.

Having bounded your study, you then have to decide which data collection methods you'll use. Writers such as Cohen, Manion and Morrison (2011) argue that to describe a situation in depth you will almost certainly have to undertake some observations, and augment these with questionnaires and/or interviews.

 Warning: The need to use multiple data collection methods and provide a detailed description of the instance under examination will reduce the number of words that you have for analysis of your data. Therefore, it's essential that your research is focused very tightly on a single, clearly defined instance.

6.8 Action research

There are a number of different interpretations of the action research strategy. The term was first used by the American academic Kurt Lewin. He was interested in exploring strategies for social change and his action research approach was underpinned by the principle of planning and implementing a social change followed by evaluation. However, the 'British tradition' is one of practice or practitioner-based research with the goal of improved professional practice.

One of the key criteria for using action research as a model for professional development is that it should have an impact on practice. Action research practitioners are, therefore, encouraged to share their findings with other professionals and this is often included as one of the assessment criteria. This sharing of good practice is intended to spread out like ripples on a pond and have a positive impact on others within the institution where the research took place/you work in. Indeed, the core of action research is that it's a social process which involves the whole 'community' in which the research takes place.

 Remember: The danger of researcher bias in action research is very high.

Therefore, to ensure that your final results are valid you have to undertake rigorous self-evaluation throughout the project. It's essential that this critical evaluation be ongoing and not just something you do at the end of the project.

Action research is a cyclical process that starts with identifying a problem. For example, if you wanted to improve boys' achievement in reading, you would start by establishing exactly what standard they were working at. You could do this by collecting assessment scores and recording your own evaluations of the boys' standard of reading. You then collect data from the children and other teachers using interviews, observations or questionnaires to try to identify the problems. This is called *baseline data*.

Your job as researcher is to reflect on the data collected and design a series of changes or *interventions* in how, say, boys are taught to read in your target group. You then implement a single small change, monitor it and assess what impact it had. If it improved the situation you continue to use it. If it made matters worse you dispense with it. Only after you have evaluated the effect of the change do you implement another small change. You keep going through this cycle until you are satisfied with the boys' level of achievement (see Handout 6.1).

6.9 Surveys

A survey involves collecting data from a large number of people in the hope that you can identify what is going on. Data can be collected from either the entire *population* that you are researching or a *sample* of them, and you'd usually collect the data at a single point in time.

 Key point: A survey can be used as your main data collection strategy, as part of a case study or as a way of collecting baseline data to be used in the design of a future research project.

Data can be collected from everyone in the population (group) you are researching or, more commonly, from a sample of the population. There are various types of sampling approaches that you can use, including the following:

- Random sampling, which ensures that every member of the population you are researching has an equal chance of being selected, e.g. names drawn from a hat.
- Stratified sampling, which involves selecting respondents from different levels or parts of the population, e.g. you might wish to interview three teachers, two Heads of Year and two Assistant Heads.
- Purposive sampling, which is probably the most useful for those undertaking a small-scale piece of qualitative research, as you select respondents who you believe have specific knowledge that will help you answer your research questions.
- Convenience sampling, which, as its name indicates, involves grabbing hold of any passer-by and collecting information from them. It smacks of laziness so I don't recommend its use except where there is no other alternative.

Among the data collection tools you might use in surveys are questionnaires, interviews and observations (see Chapter 7). Questionnaires are particularly useful for larger samples, as they can be structured for easy analysis and are straightforward to administer (see 7.6).

Interviews can be used where your sample is small and you want to explore an issue in greater depth than is allowed by a questionnaire. However, they are more difficult to analyse than questionnaires and respondent bias may creep in because people give answers that they think will please the interviewer (see 6.11).

Observations can also be a powerful data collection tool. The researcher can use either **participant observation** or **non-participant observation**. However, bias can be an issue if the researcher knows the group that is being observed, and just the presence of a non-participant observer can change how people act.

 Key point: Observations have one single advantage over questionnaires and interviews – they reveal what people actually do and not just what they say they do (see 7.3 and 7.6).

6.10 Experiments and quasi-experiments

Experiments and quasi-experiments originated in the positive/scientific paradigms but they can be used in social research as well. The difference between experiments and quasi-experiments is important. In a scientific experiment the researcher tries to identify all the variables that are at play in a process and then either removes a variable, adds a variable or changes a variable and records the results that occur. For example, a typical experiment for a drugs trial would involve identifying a group of patients who were all at a similar stage of specific disease. Half of the patients would be given the new drug and the remaining half, the control group, would be given a placebo. Doctors would then monitor the progress of the disease in both groups and from that information decide how effective the drug was.

However, in education it would be almost impossible to have a control group, because groups of people don't share the same characteristics. Every class is different. So you couldn't have a control group, because the groups wouldn't 'match up'. Nor could you use two different teaching methods on the same group and assess which is best, because you'd have to teach the same topic (a key variable in the research) to the same group using each method. Obviously, once you'd covered the topic using method A, the group's understanding of, and level of interest in, the subject would change and this would be reflected in how they reacted to method B. So, any comparison would be undermined straightaway.

Quasi-experiments don't seek to exercise the same level of control over the variables. For example, you could teach, say, *Romeo and Juliet* to a class using one teaching method and adopt another when you look at, say, *A Midsummer Night's Dream* and then evaluate the results of both methods. It's not a scientific experiment, but it would still give you a good insight into which was the most effective teaching method with that group of learners.

 Hint: Teachers undertake quasi-experiments all the time – but they call it trial and error.

SPACE FOR YOUR NOTES

6.11 Key terms

In addition to discussing your research philosophy, methodology and strategy, you will also need to define a number of key research terms and how you have dealt with the issues they seek to address. Therefore, you'll be required to write a paragraph or two on bias, ***generalisability***, ***relatability***, ethics, data protection, validity, reliability and triangulation as they relate to your research. Each of these terms is discussed below.

Bias is always present in any piece of research and it doesn't necessarily come from people with extreme views. In anti-positivist/qualitative research bias starts with your choice of topic. What you choose to research says something about your own interests and what you think is important. Therefore, it's virtually impossible for the social science researcher to come to a topic without some prior knowledge or opinion about the issues involved. In all probability it's that prior knowledge/personal interest which has attracted them to the topic. Effectively, it is not possible for the researcher to come to the research with an 'empty mind'. The best they can hope for is an 'open mind'.

The past history of the researcher can even affect quantitative researchers where they can unconsciously select particular samples and/or analyse data in a specific way which favours a particular result.

Remember: Bias can't be eliminated, however. As a researcher you have to try and identify where it exists and then minimise the impact that it will have on your research.

To deal with your own bias and that of your participants you should:

- Recognise that whatever you write will contain an element of bias.
- Demonstrate how you've attempted to counter your own bias by using a good range of writers in your literature review, some of whom you agree with and others you don't.
- When analysing the data, look for alternative interpretations, especially if the findings confirm your own views. This is particularly important at Masters level. Very rarely does data have only one interpretation. Try to challenge your own interpretations.
- Explain to the reader how you carried out your research, analysed your data, and your thinking behind the key decisions that you made. This is part of the **audit trail** that you should include as part of your work. This will enable the reader to judge for themselves to what extent your findings and interpretations are a reasonable representation of the situation.

Ethical considerations should always be at the heart of your research. Since a number of medical scandals in the 1990s there has been an increased emphasis on the need for all researchers to demonstrate that their research is ethical and will not harm the participants.

To find out what is required, have a look at the British Educational Research Association web site, www.bera.ac.uk. They publish a set of ethical guidelines that education researchers should follow. The main ones that you need to consider are:

- Do no harm. You should never undertake research that can harm the participants physically, mentally or emotionally. That's why your project/dissertation has to be approved before you can start to collect data. If during your research a participant should become distressed, you must suspend your research and discuss the issue with your supervisor.

- When dealing with children or vulnerable adults you need to be very careful, as there are specific legal obligations and, in particular, permission for the child to partake in the research must be obtained from their parents or other responsible adult. Fortunately, the general position is that permission from parents or guardians isn't necessary if the research is part of the researcher's normal professional role. So gathering assessment data on students' work or the evaluation of lessons is usually acceptable. But it's vital to check with the head of the establishment in which the research is to be carried out that these approvals are on file.

- You also need to ensure that you comply with the legal requirements for working with children and vulnerable adults; this usually means having the appropriate enhanced CRB check. It can take anything between six weeks and six months to obtain a CRB certificate. If you are an overseas student you should raise this issue at the interview stage and ask what strategies the universities have in place to support overseas students, either to obtain the certificate or design research projects that will not require the student to obtain a certificate.

- Linked to the above concept is obtaining **informed consent**. You must explain to all your participants the nature and purpose of your research and emphasise that they are under no obligation to take part in the research and that they can withdraw from it at any stage. No participant should feel coerced into taking part. This is particularly difficult for teachers when they are researching their own pupils. For example, if you give your class a questionnaire to complete they're likely to believe that they must complete it. You must explain to them their rights.

- It is important to offer all participants **anonymity** and you must make it clear that their identity will not be revealed either by naming them or using a piece of information or data that only they could have provided, e.g. if the school has four maths teachers, three of whom are in their twenties, it will be obvious whom you speaking of if you say, 'One maths teacher who has worked at the school for over 20 years said ... '.

Data protection is a good example of both a legal and an ethical requirement. You should only hold data necessary for the research and it must be disposed of in a secure way as soon as possible. Unlike the British Secret Service, who have a propensity to leave sensitive material on buses, trains and tubes, be particularly careful with data on laptops and memory sticks and don't lose them or leave them lying about. You should also securely shred all notes and transcripts written as part of the research.

Generalisability and relatability. Generalisability relates to how far your findings are applicable across the board. For example, if you were researching teaching methods in an inner-city school in Birmingham, you need to ask yourself 'To what extent are my findings applicable to all secondary schools in England?' Clearly there are limitations. The problems faced by the school, the social and ethnic mix of the students and the resources available are going to be different to those available to a teacher in a leafy Kent suburb where many of the children come from very affluent families.

 Warning: Despite the differences between an inner-city school in Birmingham and one in leafy Kent, the findings may well be of interest to the teachers in Kent. Why? Because while there will be differences, many of the same issues will be present in most settings as human nature remains remarkably consistent across social groups.

However, if you undertook a large-scale quantitative project, the results may well be generalisable provided that the sample you selected was sufficiently large/representative of whatever group or population you were looking at. But you won't have the time or resources to carry out such a survey on your Masters.

Validity and reliability. Validity is concerned with ensuring that you actually measure what you intended to measure. For example, if you are collecting data on teaching methods, how can you be certain that you are measuring the effectiveness of the method and not the engagement of the students with a particularly interesting subject or the absence of the class clown, which means that behaviour and the attention of the other students is better?

 Key point: Some aspects of your approach will be more valid or more secure than others. Your task will be to comment on which aspects are more or less valid and what could be done to improve validity.

Once you've explained how you dealt with validity you can look at its partner, reliability. Reliability is concerned with the question, 'To what extent would I get the same results if I were to repeat the research again?' With a (realist ontology) scientific experiment it's possible to get the same result time after time. But you can't interview the same person twice and expect exactly the same answers. And if you change the people you interview, you will definitely get different answers.

It is not possible to achieve the same 100 per cent reliability in qualitative research. Instead you aim to provide transparency. You describe how you carried out your research in sufficient detail to enable others to repeat your work if they wished to. You provide what is known as an 'audit trail'. For example, you will need to explain how you drew up and tested your questionnaire, how you selected and approached your respondents and exactly how the questionnaire was administered and analysed. By providing this information the reader can make a judgement about how rigorous your research has been and how reasonable your interpretation of the data has been. They could even repeat your research if they wished to confirm or refute its findings.

Triangulation involves examining an issue from more than one viewpoint. If you look at an object from just one angle you only see one aspect or surface of it. If you look at it from different angles, previously unseen features often come into focus. There are a number of different ways by which you can achieve triangulation. They include:

- Methodological triangulation, which involves the use of different methodologies, such as quantitative and qualitative, to get a fix on the situation. Using a mixed methodology approach you could compare and contrast what a teacher says in an interview (qualitative data) about improving performance with the school's SAT results from the last five years (quantitative data). In this way you're collecting data from two sources, each of which is underpinned by a different research methodology.
- Methods triangulation is by far the most popular approach used by sole researchers. Basically, the researcher uses two or more data collection methods to cross-check the data. For example, you might interview a group of teachers about the teaching methods that they use and compare this with your findings from classroom observation. One method reveals what the teachers say they do and the second what they actually do. The two may well be the same, but you would be surprised how often they differ.
- Data source triangulation involves collecting data on the same topic from different groups of participants. For example, you could collect data from teachers and children. This would give you a more rounded picture of the issue.
- Time-lapsed triangulation involves collecting data at different times or more than once from the same group of participants. This allows you to pick up on any changes in what people have to say as a result of the passage of time and the development of their ideas.
- Multiple-researcher triangulation involves more than one researcher collecting data. This does minimise the bias of any one researcher but unfortunately, by its very nature, it's not an approach that sole researchers can use.

 Hint: It's a common misunderstanding that you have to use three methods to triangulate data. The subject of the research provides one point of the triangle while the two data collection methods provide the other two.

For most small-scale research projects you'll use only one or two approaches. The most common are methods triangulation and data-source triangulation. If you use either of these approaches you gain a more complete picture of the issue that you are investigating and improve the accuracy of the data collected.

 Warning: You would not achieve triangulation by interviewing a group of teachers and then issuing them a questionnaire to complete. Why? Because in both interviews and questionnaires people tell you what they do. Only observations reveal what they actually do.

SPACE FOR YOUR NOTES

6.12 Writing your methodology section

Key point: The students who write good methodology sections are those that take the time to understand the basic principles that underpin research. It's essential that you do this before you finalise your choice of research topic and research approach. Only then can you make a truly informed choice about what it is you wish to research and how you will undertake the work.

Warning: A great idea for a piece of research plus no clear idea of how you will carry out the research equals a poor result every time.

Therefore, when you start your course your first purchases should be a book on educa- tion research. This should be your prime research textbook. However, just as you need a range of literature to produce a well-argued and critical literature review, you need to back up your core research book with a range of other texts. There is an extended list of books at the end of this chapter to choose from. However, just because I've recommended cer- tain books doesn't mean they are right for you. If at all possible, have a look at the texts in the university library before buying the one or two books which will form your core texts.

Warning: In 1.2 I spoke of the need never to discuss an idea or theory unless you understood it fully. There are more opportunities in the research methodology section to 'get it' wrong than in any other part of an assignment. Therefore, ensure that you fully understand each term that you use before you write about it.

If I have given the impression that all you have to do is write in abstract terms about your choice of research philosophy, methodology and strategies, I apologise. While it is essential that you define and explain the various issues in academic terms, you also have to explain and justify why you have selected a particular approach over another. In other words you have to show why the research philosophy, methodology and strategies were the best ones to use for your particular research.

Warning: It is not sufficient to discuss your methodology in abstract terms. You must constantly justify your choices in terms of the actual research you undertook, e.g. 'I used a qualitative approach because . . . '.

6.13 Conclusion

Of all the skills that you learn on a Masters-level course I genuinely believe that the most valuable are those which are developed through research, i.e. identification, exploration and understanding of an issue, which in turn enables you to take appropriate action to resolve a problem or improve the current situation. It is these skills that every organisation is looking for in its staff – especially those who have a management role in the organisation.

Remember: In any piece of research you have to demonstrate three things:

- An ability to undertake successfully a piece of research.
- An understanding of the theory of research.
- An ability to justify your choice of research methodology, strategy and data collection tools.

SPACE FOR YOUR NOTES

Further reading

British Educational Research Association, <http://www.bera.ac.uk>.
Cohen, L., Manion, L. and Morrison, K. (2011) *Research Methods in Education* (7th ed.). Abingdon: Routledge.
Denscombe, M. (2014) *The Good Research Guide: For Small-Scale Research Projects* (5th ed.). Berkshire: OUP/McGraw-Hill.
McGrath, J. and Coles, A. (2013) *Your Education Research Project Companion* (2nd ed.). Abingdon: Routledge.
Pring, R. (2003) Different kinds of research and their philosophical foundations, in *Philosophy of Educational Research*. London: Continuum, Ch. 3.

HANDOUT 6.1 A quick guide to choosing your research strategy

A quick guide to deciding your research strategy

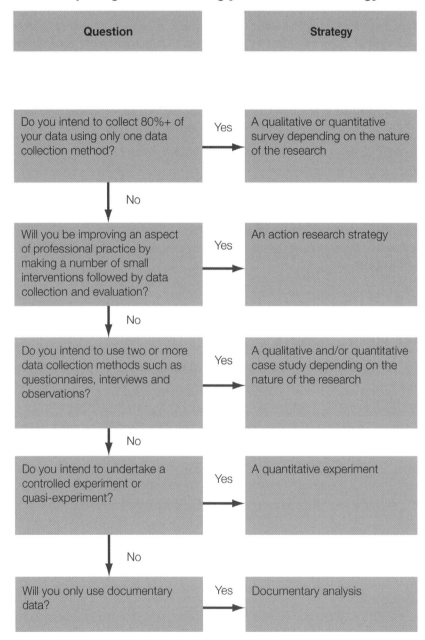

Question	Strategy
Do you intend to collect 80%+ of your data using only one data collection method? — **Yes** →	A qualitative or quantitative survey depending on the nature of the research
↓ **No**	
Will you be improving an aspect of professional practice by making a number of small interventions followed by data collection and evaluation? — **Yes** →	An action research strategy
↓ **No**	
Do you intend to use two or more data collection methods such as questionnaires, interviews and observations? — **Yes** →	A qualitative and/or quantitative case study depending on the nature of the research
↓ **No**	
Do you intend to undertake a controlled experiment or quasi-experiment? — **Yes** →	A quantitative experiment
↓ **No**	
Will you only use documentary data? — **Yes** →	Documentary analysis

(McGrath, J. and Coles, A. (2013) *Your Education Research Project Companion* (2nd ed.). Abingdon: Routledge, p. 124.)

7 Data collection tools

Interviews, observations and questionnaires

> **Aim of chapter:** To enable you to choose the right data collection tools for your research.
>
> **Chapter overview:** This chapter discusses the three most popular data collection tools available to Masters students, i.e. interviews, observations and questionnaires, and when each can be used to maximum effect. It is shown that each tool can be categorised as either closed, open or semi-structured depending on the nature of the questions asked or the range of events itemised prior to an observation. The use of participant and non-participant observations is also discussed and advice given on how to ensure that a data collection tool will actually collect the data required to answer the listed research questions.

7.1 Introduction

 Key point: The quality of your final assignment is dependent on the quality of the data you collect.

This chapter introduces you to the three most popular data collection tools in education research, namely, interviews, observations and questionnaires. It's likely that you will be familiar with these methods from previous studies. As with Chapter 6 this overview is intended to give you a flavour of what you will find yourself involved with when studying for your Masters. It is not intended to provide the definitive guide to the tools discussed and the difficulties that unwary researchers can encounter when they fail to understand the nature, purpose and limitations of these tools.

7.2 Arranging an interview or observation and agreeing the ground rules

To successfully complete a research project you need a certain amount of administrative skills, not least of which is the ability to organise appointments and venues for interviews and observations.

 Remember: Anyone who agrees to be interviewed or observed is doing you a favour. Therefore, treat them with consideration and respect.

If you want to interview or observe someone, make personal contact with them and explain the purpose of your research before you send out the official request. If possible, meet them in person. Failing that, speak to them on the phone. If that is not possible, contact them by email and introduce yourself. If they are willing to be involved, follow up your conversation or email with a detailed letter or email confirming the nature of the research and the conditions upon which they are taking part. The conditions should include a commitment on your part to maintain the person's anonymity and a clear statement telling them that they can withdraw from the research at any time should they wish to do so. Also include details of the date, time and venue for the interview or observation and an indication of how long the session will last. And finally, explain to them how they can access a copy of the completed research should they wish to read it.

Always try to see the person on their 'turf' not yours, and if that's not possible, on neutral ground. It's a matter of putting them at their ease and limiting any fears or nerves that they might have.

Although views differ on this, I would always send a copy of the interview questions or observation schedule to the respondent in advance of any interview or observation. It gives the person a chance to think about the types of issues that you're interested in. But other writers and many students don't agree with me. They think that if you tell respondents what you're looking for in advance it gives them the chance to prepare an answer or change their behaviour. While in theory that's true, in reality I believe people are too busy to prepare an answer in advance or to plan a change in their behaviour just for you.

 Remember: Always maintain the anonymity of your respondents but never promise them **confidentiality**. Why? Because you intend to write about what they tell you!

During or after an interview people will often tell you something 'in confidence'. Obviously, you can't divulge such information unless you have a legal obligation, such as child protection concerns. I once had a respondent who, at the end of the interview, leant across the desk and in a whisper said, 'Now I'll tell you what I really think about the principal'; it was great data but I couldn't use it because it was told to me in confidence.

7.3 Types of interviews and when to use them

The type of interview that you conduct is determined by what you want to find out and the people that you intend to interview. But you also have to take into account the time that you have available and the word limit on your assignment. You have to be practical. The types of interviews and observations available to you can be plotted on a continuum that runs from **structured** to completely **unstructured**. And in the middle you have **semi-structured**. This is summarised in Table 7.1 below.

In a completely structured interview you'd have a long list of closed questions, such as name, age, gender, job title, length of time in present post, educational experience, etc., and your questions would be very specific. While such an approach is more like a questionnaire than an interview, it's an interview because you are sitting in front of the person asking the questions. It would be described as 'highly structured' because, as the interviewer, you've

Table 7.1 Continuum of interviews and observations

Approach	Examples	Strengths	Weaknesses
Highly structured: The researcher determines in advance what information they wish to collect.	Questions/ categories are pre-specified in detail and allow for only specific answers, e.g. yes, no, age, agree, disagree, behaviour seen/not seen, count.	Data analysis is simplified.	The researcher's view of what is important dominates data collected and restrains respondent from expressing their views.
Semi-structured: The researcher knows the broad headings that they wish to collect data on but is open to the unexpected provided it is relevant to their research.	Questions/ categories are broader. Questions and observation prompts are seen as the starting point for the collection of data rather than the end.	Reduced researcher bias. The respondents' actions or words are used to determine what is important. This increases the likelihood that data new to the researcher will be uncovered.	Increased variability in the issues covered leading to increased problems of comparability and data analysis.
Unstructured: The researcher has an interest in a particular issue but does not wish to limit the research to parameters that they impose, either arbitrarily or because of their lack of knowledge.	Questions are broad and open-ended. Observation schedules may be 'blank' or composed of just a few prompts.	Researcher bias is minimised and the range of issues identified expanded very significantly.	Comparability between data-sets is significantly decreased, making analysis much more difficult and time-consuming.

decided the parameters of the discussion in advance, and the type of question you're asking requires specific information from the respondent, which means that they can't digress from your agenda.

While it may be boring, the structured interview can be used instead of a questionnaire when you're dealing with children or people who either can't read or can't understand a questionnaire, or with any group that is likely to provide a poor response rate. By their nature, structured interviews produce specific information and may not on their own produce enough data for many small-scale projects.

At the other end of the continuum you have the completely unstructured interview, where you sit down and say something like 'Tell me about your experience as a teacher'. That's a very open question and it invites the respondent to tell you whatever they think is important about their experiences. However, such an approach runs the risk of producing vast amounts of unusable data. Very few small-scale research projects use this approach because of the time it takes to carry out the interviews and analyse the data obtained.

The unstructured interview is really useful when you're investigating a new topic and want to find out about the major themes and ideas contained within it. You may decide to hold one or two unstructured interviews, then having discovered the main themes you might devise a semi-structured interview schedule to delve deeper into the issues you are interested in. They are also invaluable when you're undertaking an in-depth study of people's experiences over an extended period of time – for example, their experiences at school. However, unstructured interviews produce masses of data, which take time to write up and analyse.

Semi-structured interviews sit in the middle of the continuum. Which is why most single researchers use them. The researcher knows the broad areas on which they wish to collect information and they ask a series of open-ended questions that cover just these areas.

 Warning: A 30-minute, semi-structured interview will generate about six pages of single-spaced A4 text. That amounts to about 18,000 words of data for six interviews. That's way in excess of the word limit for most assignments. Therefore, agree with your supervisor the number of interviews you will undertake and their length.

Semi-structured interviews are the most popular with sole researchers. They are used when the researcher is aware of the main issues surrounding their topic and they have a clear idea of what data they want to collect. The questions are designed to be open-ended and allow the respondent to talk about issues in reasonable depth but within a framework designated by the researcher. The result is that the information collected is usually relevant and reasonably easy to analyse.

Interviews are ideal for exploring people's attitudes, beliefs, perceptions, opinions etc. in depth. However, it's worth remembering that while interviews tell you what people think they do, they do not reveal what the person actually does. Very often there is a mismatch between what someone says they do and what they actually do. That's why it's so valuable to check what a person says by undertaking observations. This is an example of methods triangulation (see 6.11).

The type of interview that you conduct is determined by what you want to find out and the people that you intend to interview. But you also have to take into account the time that you have available and the word limit on your assignment. You have to be practical.

 Hint: Whichever type of interview you use, pilot it first to confirm that it collects the information you need (see Handout 7.1).

SPACE FOR YOUR NOTES

7.4 Participant and non-participant observations

As indicated above, very often people are unaware that there's a difference between what they say they do and what they actually do. For example, it is not unusual for teachers to describe their teaching style as '*learner-centred*'. But when you observe them, they use *teacher-centred* methods most of the time.

 Key point: To find out what's actually happening you need to do some observations.

However, it's difficult to get people to act naturally if they know they're being observed. That's why there are two types of observation: participant and non-participant. An Ofsted inspector who sits at the back of the class watching you teach is using non-participant observation. They're alien to the classroom and don't take part in the lesson. Their presence changes the behaviour of both the teacher and the children. Participant observation occurs when the researcher collects data at the same time as they engage in their normal activities. For example, while teaching a class the teacher may also observe how learners react to certain teaching methods. She doesn't record her findings in the class but waits until the end of the lesson and then writes her notes up.

At first glance, participant observation seems to contradict the cardinal ethical requirement that that you obtain informed consent from all participants. To overcome this potential problem, discuss the research in advance with the participants and obtain their approval in the normal way (see 7.2). Then, to eliminate the risk that they might act differently, leave it for a week or two before you do the observation. By then, they've forgotten about your research and have reverted to acting normally.

 Hint: If you want to know what actually happens during the normal flow of work use participant observation.

7.5 Types of observations and when to use them

As with interviews, observations can be highly structured, semi-structured or unstructured. A structured observation requires a very detailed observation schedule to be drawn up. When an event occurs the researcher places an x against the appropriate category. However, the sheer complexity of what is going on means it can be very difficult to capture every detail and you may wish to consider using a second researcher to help you. Or you might video the event or undertake more than one observation of the group/individual you're observing.

Unstructured observations require nothing more than a blank sheet of paper on which the researcher records what they have seen using either notes or a **mind map**. As with unstructured interviews, they are used when you have very little idea of what actually takes place during the event being observed. However, I know from personal experience just how difficult it is to carry out an unstructured observation. Therefore, I'd suggest that you observe an example of the event you wish to research and, based upon that, draw up and administer a semi-structured observation schedule.

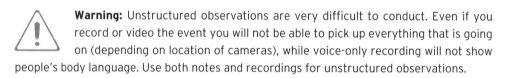 **Warning:** Unstructured observations are very difficult to conduct. Even if you record or video the event you will not be able to pick up everything that is going on (depending on location of cameras), while voice-only recording will not show people's body language. Use both notes and recordings for unstructured observations.

A semi-structured observation schedule lists a number of key events that the researcher expects to see but leaves room for the unexpected to be recorded. As with semi-structured interviews, they are the most popular choice for the sole researcher and are used when the researcher has a good idea of what events they expect to see but leave space to record the unexpected.

7.6 Questionnaires and when to use them

Previously I said that interviews and observations could be located on a continuum from highly structured to completely unstructured (see 7.3). Well, questionnaires can also fit onto that continuum. You could have a highly structured questionnaire that only asked closed questions, such as age, gender, etc., or you could have one that asked people to write about their views on a particular subject.

However, I don't think that you'd get many responses from a totally unstructured questionnaire. It would take too long to complete, which is why they are very seldom used. Research seems to indicate that if a questionnaire can't be completed in 6 to 8 minutes, most people throw it in the bin. Of course, if you give your respondents some inducement, such as a bottle of wine or free shopping vouchers, they may be willing to spend longer on the task.

However, a fear that people may not complete your questionnaire does not mean that you can only ask closed questions. A well-designed questionnaire should contain a mixture of open and closed questions. Table 7.2 summarises the most popular types of questions that education researchers use.

Table 7.2 Types of questions found in a questionnaire

Question type	Example
Closed	Please state your: Name Age Gender
Range	Please indicate how old you are: 20-29, 30-39, 40-49, 50-59, 60 and over. Note: Don't make the following common mistake. Please indicate how old you are: 20-30, 30-40, 40-50, etc.
Multiple-choice	Which of the following statements is untrue? Tick one only: During the 1970s Margaret Thatcher was the Minister for Education. ☐ Margaret Thatcher was forced to resign as Prime Minister when she failed to decisively defeat Michael Heseltine when he stood for leadership of the Conservative Party in 1990. ☐ Tony Blair succeeded Margaret Thatcher as Prime Minister in 1997. ☐
Ranking	Rank the following teaching methods in terms of your personal preference, with one being your favourite. ☐ lecture ☐ group work ☐ pair working ☐ role play ☐ team teaching ☐ discussion ☐ discovery learning ☐ student presentations
Select	Tick each of the following teaching methods that you use on a regular basis (i.e. once per week). lecture ☐ group work ☐ pair working ☐ role play ☐ discussion ☐ discovery learning ☐ student presentations ☐
Likert scale	Read the following sentence and tick the statement that best describes your reaction: Ofsted inspections help teachers to improve their professional practice. Agree strongly ☐ agree ☐ neither agree nor disagree ☐ disagree ☐ disagree strongly ☐
Semi-structured	Typically semi-structured questions ask you to write a short comment on your answer to the previous question.
Unstructured	Such questions are rarely used but typically they ask the respondent to write a paragraph in response to the question posed.

7.7 Piloting your questionnaire

While questionnaires allow you to collect a lot of data from a range of participants they are not easy to design. It's essential that once you have drawn up your questionnaire that you pilot it. Start by giving it to your tutor, colleague or critical friend first and ask them to check it for use of English and clarity of meaning. That way you can pick up on any questions that are ambiguous. Then amend it in the light of any feedback that they gave you. Only then should you pilot it with a representative sample of your intended participants.

If you are wondering why you have to pilot your questionnaire with tutor/colleague/critical friend and a sample of respondents it's because while 'someone in education' may understand your questionnaire it doesn't mean that a child or parent will. Non-educationalists can be confused by the jargon and type of language used. You should also check how long it takes participants to complete the questionnaire. Ensure that it can be completed within the 6- to 8-minute timescale that respondents are typically willing to spend filling one in.

Remember: Questionnaires are hard to design. They take a lot more time to develop, pilot and amend than a set of interview questions. But once completed they are much easier to analyse.

7.8 Justifying your choice of data collection methods

Key point: As with your research methodology, it isn't sufficient to just list the strengths and weaknesses of each method you used. You have to show why your choice of methods is the best fit for your particular research. Essentially you are required to produce a rationale for why you have used the tools you have and rejected others.

7.9 Conclusion

Whichever tools you use, make sure that they collect the data that you require to answer your research questions. This may seem obvious, but numerous students fail to align their research questions with their data collection tools. I suggest that you carry out a cross-check between your research question and **research tool** prior to its use to ensure that you are collecting all the information you require (see Handout 7.1).

SPACE FOR YOUR NOTES

Further reading

Cohen, L., Manion, L. and Morrison, K. (2011) *Research Methods in Education Paperback* (7th ed.). Abingdon: Routledge.

Denscombe, M. (2014) *The Good Research Guide: For Small-Scale Research Projects* (5th ed.). Berkshire: OUP/McGraw-Hill.

McGrath, J. and Coles, A. (2013) *Your Education Research Project Companion* (2nd ed.). Abingdon: Routledge.

HANDOUT 7.1 Collecting the data required to answer your research questions

Exercise

There is nothing worse when undertaking a piece of research than to find that you have failed to collect the data you need to answer one or more of your research questions. This happens more often than you'd think. The following exercise can minimise the chance of it happening to you.

Note: You need to do this exercise before you start to collect your data.

List your research questions on the left-hand side of the page. List your interview questions, questionnaire questions or the incidents that you intend to observe on the right-hand side of the page.

Then draw a line from the first research question to the questions or incidents that you will use to collect data for that research question. Repeat this exercise for your remaining research questions.

What you are aiming for is at least one line connecting every question or activity to a research question.

DO THE EXERCISE BEFORE READING ON

If you conduct the exercise before you collect your data and find that one or more of your data collection questions or activities do not link to a research question, you need to revise your data collection tools.

If you do the exercise after you've collected your data, and you find that one or more of your data collection questions or activities are not linked to a research question, don't worry. You've just wasted time collecting data that you can't use.

However, if there is no link to one of your research questions you are in trouble. Effectively, it means that none of your questions or activities observed will provide data to help you answer that research question. It is very unlikely that you will be able to go back and collect the missing data from participants – if for no other reason than it would make you look stupid!

However, not all is lost. Examine the data you have collected and change your research questions to fit the data you've got. Sneaky, maybe, but it's the best way out of a tight spot, and your marker need never know!

8 How to structure a research report, dissertation or journal article

Aim of chapter: To provide you with guidance on how to structure a research report, dissertation or journal article and the content of each section within these documents.

Chapter overview: This chapter outlines a common structure that is used when writing a research report or dissertation. However, it emphasises that other structures are used and that the student must check which structure is favoured in their institution. The typical content of the introduction, literature review, research methodology, findings (includes analysis) and conclusion is outlined and practical advice given on writing each section. The chapter ends by discussing the growing popularity of assignments that require students to write in the style of a journal article. However, it is stressed that what is required is an assignment in the style of a journal article, not a piece of work that is of publishable standard.

8.1 Introduction

It is almost certain that you will have to produce a research report and/or a dissertation as part of your Masters studies. You may also be required to produce an assignment in the style of a journal article. For that reason, I have devoted an entire chapter to these three important methods of assessment. Chapter 9 examines presentations and essays.

Some readers may find aspects of this tutorial challenging because it introduces jargon which is commonly used in the research process. All of this jargon is defined in the glossary and in Chapters 6 and 7. If you find the chapter heavy going, I suggest you skim read it. This will provide you with an idea of what you are aiming to write. You can return to the chapter later when you are more familiar with some of the terminology used and faced with writing either a research project report or dissertation.

Most universities provide a series of taught research sessions as part of their Masters-level courses. It's important that you attend as many of these sessions as possible. During the course you will be offered advice on a suitable research topic and allocated a supervisor.

 Key point: Your supervisor will see you on a one-to-one basis for a specified number of hours. They will read your report or dissertation as you write it and do the following:

- Approve your research proposal before you commence collecting data.
- Make suggestions for what literature you might look at.
- Recommend changes to your research methodology, strategy or data collection methods as required.
- Read sections of your work and make suggestions for how they could be improved.
- Comment on your analysis of data and your interpretation of the data.

The message to remember is that you are not alone when you start your research.

Warning: Just about every Masters student initially chooses a project or dissertation which is far too large to complete in the time available and with the resources they can call upon. So, keep it simple and keep it small.

Remember: Even a dissertation is just a short story – not a Tolstoyan novel.

8.2 Structure of a dissertation or research report

The format I've outlined below for a research report or dissertation is fairly standard but there are variations on it. So check out just what your supervisor wants. Some supervisors and universities like students to write separate findings and analysis sections. Personally, I think this is a waste of words because in the analysis you will have to refer again to the findings before you can undertake any analysis. This seems to me a waste of precious words which could be better spent in actually extending the level of analysis.

Key point: There are many ways you could structure a research report or dissertation, but unless you are a genius submit the assignment in the format suggested by your supervisor/tutor.

The title. While the actual format of a report or dissertation may vary there are certain key features that appear in all reports, regardless of what they might be called. So, let's start at the beginning with the title.

Students often agonise over a title for their work. They think that it needs to tell the reader what the research is all about. However, as you will see, the abstract, which appears before the Introduction, does that far more effectively than any title ever could. Therefore, think of a title that is short, snappy and interesting. One that gives a clear indication of what the work is about but which does not try to provide a detailed outline of what you have written. Besides, if your title is totally useless/inappropriate your supervisor will tell you.

Warning: Don't get hung up over a title. Titles are important, but not that important. No one ever passed a Masters dissertation because they had a great title or failed because they had a poor title. Although one title I saw did run to half a page in length!

The front pages and abstract

 Key point: The front pages are important because they are what the reader sees first and, unfair as it may seem, first impressions count.

The front pages consist of:

- a table of contents;
- a list of all tables;
- a list of all figures;
- a list of any appendices;
- an abstract.

You are familiar with the table of contents but you must ensure that the page numbers specified are correct. It is very easy during your final editing to alter the page on which a sub-section or chapter starts. Therefore, the very last thing you check before submission should be your table of contents and page numbers, i.e. are the titles used in the body of the text the same as those in the table of contents and are the page numbers correct?

A figure is anything that is not a table and includes charts, diagrams and pictures. You should provide a separate list of all tables and figures. Each figure and table requires a title and a number, for example:

Table 8.1: Summary of Exam Results. Page 23

Abstracts are hard to write and I suggest that you leave yours until you have finished writing up your research. The abstract needs to summarise in about 200 words what the research is about and what the key issues and findings are. It is not something that you can dash off in 10 minutes. A good abstract needs to be written over several days. That does not mean that you work constantly on it 8 hours a day. Spend an hour on the first day writing a good draft then, over a week, pick it up every day for 10 or 15 minutes and see how you can change and improve it. In the time between looking at the abstract your subconscious mind will be mulling over what you have written and when you return to it the result of your conscious and unconscious reflection will come out.

 Remember: Titles are little babies crying for attention; don't expect them to do the work of their big brother/sister – the abstract.

8.3 The introduction

Key point: Introductions are important. They must set the scene for what is to come and explain clearly what the work is all about.

There are six things you need to do in the introduction:

- Describe the focus of your research.
- Outline your three research questions.
- Say why you are interested in the subject.
- Explain where the research took place and who was involved.
- Say why the research was worth doing.
- Provide a very brief outline of how the remainder of the report or dissertation is structured.

Start the Introduction with a paragraph or two that summarises what your research is about, e.g. 'In this dissertation I explore the impact that an adverse Ofsted Report has on the management and leadership of a secondary school and the reaction of staff and students to the changes that followed'. Such a paragraph straightaway tells the reader what your assignment is about.

Follow the ***focal paragraph*** with a list of your research questions. These are more specific than your focal paragraph and break your overall focus down into those constituent parts that you want to explore in detail, for example:

'Specifically, I wish to explore:

- What changes took place in the management style of the Head Teacher and Senior Management team following publication of the OfSTED Report.
- The reaction of staff to the new style of management.
- The reaction of staff and students to the criticisms contained in the Ofsted Report'.

These three research questions become the precise focus of your assignment and it is them that you will address, and nothing else. What you are doing is setting the limits of your work and, provided they are reasonable and logical, your tutor will not mark you down for failing to address an issue outside the scope of your assignment, for example, 'How did the parents of pupils react to the Ofsted Report?' is a valid question but it is not part of your research focus.

In order to orientate the reader it's essential to tell them where the research is going to take place and who your participants are going to be. This helps them to understand the context in which the research took place. Briefly describe the setting in which the research took place, e.g. was it in an inner-city school or in the leafy suburbs, how many staff and students does it have, what percentage of the learners receive free school meals or speak English as a second language? That sort of thing.

However, you must never provide any material that would identify the organisation in which the research took place or any of the research participants. It is essential that you maintain anonymity at all times (see 6.11).

Then you can tell the reader how you collected your data and who from. For example, you might say 'In order to collect my data I issued a questionnaire to all teachers in the school and held a 25-minute semi-structured interview with three senior teachers'.

Having outlined your research aims, where the work was undertaken and how you collected your data and from whom, it's time for you to say why it's worth doing. Acceptable reasons include 'I have a professional interest in the topic and/or it will help me to improve my professional practice or solve a problem at work'.

To end the introduction, briefly outline the remaining contents of the report, for example:

- 'In the literature review I critically evaluate the literature relating to teaching methods in secondary schools.
- The research methodology section outlines the reasons why I have adopted a qualitative approach and used questionnaires as my primary data collection tool.
- The findings contains a summary and analysis of the data I collected.
- The conclusion summarises the three most significant findings that I have learnt from undertaking this research, discusses weaknesses in my research and identifies areas for further study'.

 Remember: A sloppy introduction will annoy your marker and, like a certain well-known green giant, you don't want to make your marker angry.

SPACE FOR YOUR NOTES

8.4 The literature review: some dos and don'ts

Key point: A good literature review critically evaluates what writers have said – it doesn't just report what they said (see 5.7).

Start your literature review with a very short introduction that summarises how you have structured the review and the areas of literature you are going to discuss, e.g. 'This review is structured thematically, based upon the areas covered by my research questions, including . . . ' or 'As I am looking at the development of behaviour management in the classroom over the last 50 years, I have structured this review chronologically'.

Do not provide a report of a book or article, e.g. 'In their book *Surviving an Ofsted Inspection*, Beano and Dandy (2014) outline strategies that Head Teachers can adopt and suggest ways to implement them'. Such a statement is useless. What were the strategies they suggested? How should they be implemented? Tell us what the author actually said and critically evaluate their ideas (see 5.7).

Avoid using long quotes. They only prove that you can copy material out of a book – a skill which you mastered around the age of 7 or 8. Summarise the arguments in your own words and remember to reference the source of the ideas fully (see 5.10). Use short powerful quotes to emphasise a particular point that you want to make. If you're really good, you can take the arguments of two or more writers and synthesise what they say on a particular subject. *Synthesis* is a high-level academic skill and if you can do it you will earn high marks. However, many students find it a difficult concept to grasp.

Hint: To understand synthesis, think about Lego bricks. When you were a child you probably played with Lego bricks or something similar. First you built a house (think of this as the data you collected). Then you took it apart brick by brick (this is analysis). Finally you used the same bricks to build a boat (this is synthesis). Synthesis is about the reconfiguration of data and ideas and creating something new and different from existing data and/or literature.

Avoid the situation where you start every paragraph with the names of writers, e.g. 'McGrath and Coles (2013) suggest that . . . '. Such an approach gives the impression of a shopping list. Instead, summarise what McGrath and Coles say in your own words and then at the end add the reference. This simple technique makes a huge difference to how your literature review reads and gives the impression that you have internalised the message from the writer. Don't believe me – try it for yourself.

Read 5.2, 5.3 and 5.4 again and remember to only select the most appropriate literature that deals with your research topic. Except for seminal or really important books and articles, use literature that has been published in the last five or six years. If you must use older material, do so sparingly.

If you don't use a piece of literature to analyse your findings, you need to ask yourself, 'Why have I included this author in the literature review?' The theories and ideas contained in the literature review are there to help you explain, explore, confound or support your findings. If any piece of literature is not doing that, why is it in the review?

There is only one type of literature that you may need but which you don't refer to in your findings and that is background information. This information contextualises the issues and ideas you wish to discuss. For example, you might want to briefly outline government policy on school inspection before you start to explore a recent inspection in your school. Such literature is important. It stays. But keep it brief.

Remember: With all literature, either use it or lose it!

8.5 The research methodology section

Key point: If you are undertaking a piece of research, it's essential that you can explain what you did and why you did it!

Not unreasonably, the research methodology section is crucial to any piece of research. In it you have to demonstrate that you're a competent researcher and that you understand a range of research methodologies, strategies and data collection tools, and a range of issues associated with carrying out research (see Chapters 6 and 7).

Start the section with a statement similar to the following: 'The research philosophy I adopted was largely **anti-positivist**. The research methodology that I applied was **qualitative** in nature, the research strategy was that of a **case study**, the methods used to collect data included **observation**, **questionnaires** and **semi-structured interviews**'.

Warning: I'm not suggesting that you have to use the above philosophies, methodologies, strategies and methods. I am only suggesting that you summarise your approach in a similar short paragraph, substituting the words in bold for whatever you used.

Take each of the words or phrases shown in bold and critically evaluate them (itemise their strengths and weaknesses) in terms of your research. This last phrase is vital. A simple list of strengths and weaknesses won't do. You have to explain what their strengths and weaknesses are in terms of your research (see 6.12 and 7.8).

Remember: Use the above approach like a maths formula and replace the words in bold with terms that are relevant to your research.

Having discussed your research methodology, strategy and methods, you need to explain how you have dealt with issues of bias, ethics, data protection, generalisability, relatability, validity, reliability and triangulation in your research. Allocate one or two paragraphs to each concept and start by defining what each means before outlining how you have dealt with it in your research.

To conclude the chapter, outline what you actually did and any problems that you encountered.

 Remember: As with the literature review, you should not rely on just one textbook to inform your methodology section. While it's okay to use one book as your main resource, you need to supplement it with a couple of more references (see Further Reading in Chapters 6 and 7).

8.6 The findings and analysis

 Key point: The findings and conclusion sections are the crux of any research assignment. They represent the creative element of your work and, as such, they should account for a minimum of 50 per cent of the work.

The remaining 50 per cent can be split as follows:

- 5 per cent for the abstract and introduction;
- 25 per cent for the literature review;
- 20 per cent for the research methodology.

These are a guideline only and your research may differ. But if you find that only 20 per cent of your assignment is given over to the findings and conclusions there's something seriously wrong!

As with the previous sections, start your findings by explaining the structure and content of the section. I would suggest that you use your research questions, suitably amended, as subheadings. This will prove a mirror image of what you did in the literature review and help you check that all the relevant literature is used in your analysis of the data.

Adopt a three-stage approach to the analysis of your data, i.e.:

- Describe/report your data.
- Analyse your data using the theories and ideas contained in your literature review, e.g. 'As Beano (2015) predicted I found that . . . ' or, conversely, 'In contrast to Dandy (2015) I found no evidence for his claim that . . . '. Effectively, what you are trying to do is test your findings against the extant literature. In this way you use it to explain, explore, support and challenge your findings.
- Analyse your data by comparing one piece of data with another, i.e. does data B support or refute your interpretation of what data A means? This cross-checking allows you to support the claims you make for your own interpretation of data and enables you to challenge what other researchers/writers may have said.

It's good practice to follow Hayek's advice and present the strongest argument you can against your own views and then demonstrate why your arguments are superior. This is difficult, but it's also what distinguishes good academic work from the average.

8.7 Writing your conclusions

 Key point: Just as you need a strong start, you need a strong finish. It's the last thing your marker reads before they start to write up your mark sheet. So leave them with a positive impression.

No new literature or findings can be introduced at this stage. Let me say that again: **No new literature or findings can be introduced at this stage.**

It's essential that your conclusions flow naturally from your findings, so make sure that there's coherence between what you say in the findings and what you discuss in the conclusions. You would be surprised how often the two don't match up.

 Hint: Use the Rule of Three to write your conclusions, i.e.:

- List your three main findings.
- Discuss any weaknesses in your research.
- List areas for future possible research.

Discuss the three major findings that have emerged from your work. These may be issues that have surprised you or are going to influence your future professional practice and/or thinking.

Discuss any weaknesses in your research and how you have attempted to deal with it. Many students feel that it's dangerous to reveal their weaknesses/errors and that they will lose marks for it. Not so. Your marker will see the weakness in your work far more clearly than you. What they want to see is that you also recognised the weaknesses. One very good student I had made a mess of some analysis and on reading it I realised she wouldn't get the Distinction that she and I both expected. However, in the conclusion she explained how the error had occurred and why it was not possible to put it right and how she would avoid such an error in the future. Her mark went back up to 70 per cent-plus.

Conclusions are essentially discursive and, therefore, there is no place for any recommendations. If you want to make recommendations, you require an additional section. But exercise some restraint on your ego. There is not much point in recommending that the government change its policy because of the research you have done. They're not going to read your dissertation. I've seen such recommendations made a few times on very weak dissertations. Such grandiose thinking does make me cringe and confirms that a very small percentage of students are in need of a reality check.

8.8 Assignments in the form of a journal article

 Key point: If you have to write an assignment in the form of a journal article, don't panic. **You are not required to write an article that is of publishable standard**. You are only required to write an article in the **STYLE** of a journal article. So stop worrying. You can do it.

If you look at five journal articles, you will find that they are all differ in terms of layout. There is no standard format for a journal article. However, the vast majority will contain an abstract, an introduction, findings and analysis (often called the discussion or something similar) and a conclusion. You will notice that the literature review and research methodology sections are missing from the above list. Some articles will have a separate literature review, but as often as not the review will form part of the discussion. Similarly, it is rare in education articles to find a full explanation of how the research was carried out.

The best strategy for you to adopt is to find a peer-reviewed article that you like and which is of similar length to your assignment, and analyse how it has been structured/laid out. Use this format as the template for your assignment. Just in case your marker doesn't like the format, you should state on the acknowledgements page, which appears as one of the front papers, which article you based the layout on.

In addition to following the layout of your chosen article you should also look at the style that the writer adopts. Their style will be assertive, as they are trying to convince the reader of their findings. You need to adopt a similar assertive style if possible. Don't try and copy the author's precise style; simply look at what you write and ask yourself 'Can I say that more clearly and/or forcefully?'

8.9 Conclusion

You will be provided with guidance on how to write your research report and/or dissertation by tutors and supervisors. Guidance will also be provided by the academic support team, library staff, the module handbook and the student handbook. Use one or all of them!

Having accessed the above, if you are still having a problem, speak to your supervisor again. They are ultimately responsible for your work on any research project or dissertation. They will help you if they can.

SPACE FOR YOUR NOTES

Further reading

Biggam, J. (2011) *Succeeding with Your Masters Dissertation: A Step-by-Step Handbook* (2nd ed.). Berkshire: OUP/McGraw-Hill.

McGrath, J. and Coles, A. (2013) *Your Education Research Project Companion* (2nd ed.). Abingdon: Routledge, Ch. 3 and 10.

HANDOUT 8.1　Format of a dissertation or research report

Dissertation and project guidance and structure

1. **Title**
2. **Table of contents**

- List of tables
- List of figures
- List of appendices
- Acknowledgements (Optional)
- Dedication (Optional)

---

3. **Abstract (200 words)**
4. **Introduction (5 per cent)**

- Define the question or scope of the topic that you are writing about.
- From the focus, draw out a maximum of three research questions. If you have more questions, the depth of your answers will suffer.
- Contextualise the research. Describe where, how and with whom you will carry out the research. Maintain the organisation's and participants' anonymity.
- Explain why the research is worth doing.
- Outline the remaining content of the assignment.

---

5. **Review of literature (25 per cent)**

- Introduce the section by briefly outlining the main areas of literature that will be discussed in the review.
- Remember that you are undertaking a critical review of the literature and not just repeating what you have read.
- Reference material correctly – see the student handbook and/or the library services guide to writing references.
- Avoid using excessively long quotes. A summary of a writer's opinions, in your own words, is more valuable than a long quote – anyone can copy from a book.
- Check that the material is relevant. If you don't use it to explain/explore your findings, why include it?

---

6. Research methodology (20 per cent)

The research methodology section is a crucial element of your assignment and one that people often find difficult. This note suggests one way that you might structure the section – it does not claim to be the only way!

Start with a summary of the research approach that you adopted, e.g. 'The research philosophy that I adopted was **anti-positivist** in nature. Within the **interpretivist** paradigm I adopted a **qualitative** methodology. My research strategy was that of a **survey**, the methods used to collect data included **observation, questionnaires and semi-structured interviews**'.

Define what you mean by each of the words in bold and discuss the strengths and weaknesses associated with that approach, strategy or method and why you rejected any alternatives.

- Explain how you have dealt with:
    o bias
    o ethics
    o data protection
    o generalisability and relatability
    o triangulation
    o validity and reliability
    o the analysis of data
- Describe what you actually did and provide a timeline to guide the reader through the process you adopted.
- Provide a short conclusion that considers the strengths and weaknesses of the approach you adopted in the light of experience and what you might do differently if you had the opportunity.

7. Findings (45 per cent)

Introduce the section by briefly explaining the scope and content of the section.

- Discuss one point at a time and link the various issues you wish to discuss with linking phrases, e.g. 'In the above section I considered the motivational impact of transformational leadership. In this section I shall explore how transformational leadership can be employed to exploit staff'.
- Adopt a three-stage approach to analysing your data. Describe what you found, then analyse it using your literature review to challenge, support, and analyse your data, e.g. 'As Bloggs (19xx) predicted I found that . . . '.
- Then using your own data, provide a logical explanation of what you think the data/findings mean. Relate your findings back to issues discussed in the literature review, and always reference all material correctly.

8. Conclusions (5 per cent)

- It is essential that your conclusions flow naturally from your findings.
- No new literature or findings should be introduced at this stage.
- Detail the three most significant findings discovered.
- Outline any weaknesses in the research.
- Identify any areas of the work that would benefit from further research.

9. End papers

Some universities ask students to provide a bibliography of all the material that they read pertaining to the writing of their assignment. Most only require that you provide a list of the references that you have actually used in your assignment. Check what your university's policy is.

Include all appendices clearly marked with both a number and a title.

Points to remember

- The word count includes the abstract and everything from the first word of the introduction to the last word of the conclusion. It does not include your front papers, list of references or appendices.
- A minimum of 50 per cent of the assignment should be devoted to the findings, analysis and conclusions.
- Whenever possible, use a small word rather than a large one.
- If a sentence is longer than 20 words you probably have two or more sentences.
- Only one issue should be discussed in a single paragraph.
- Remember: *one* point = *one* paragraph.
- Keep it simple. Working at this level is all about discussing complex ideas in a simple and clear manner.

9 Presentations and written assignments

Aim of chapter: To provide you with the knowledge and skills to plan and deliver an effective presentation.

Chapter overview: This chapter outlines 15 things that every presenter should do if they wish to deliver an effective presentation. Advice includes: knowing the criteria against which the presentation will be assessed, illustrating a presentation without using the ubiquitous PowerPoint Presentation and dealing with questions from the audience/ tutor. Twelve errors to avoid are also listed including the risk that any presenter takes if they decide to start their presentation by telling a joke or amusing story. Readers are reminded of the rules of good essay writing and the key '***process words***' that examiners use are defined e.g. 'compare and contrast', 'evaluate' and 'list/enumerate'. Further advice is also provided on the process of essay writing and the use of good academic English.

9.1 Introduction

In addition to writing research reports, dissertations and 'journal articles' it is very likely that you will have to complete other types of assignments. These include presentations, essays and portfolios.

Presentations will receive the most attention. This is because they often present the greatest challenge to Masters students. A presentation is not the same as a lesson and if you treat it as such you won't achieve the results you want or expect. You need to treat your audience in a presentation as an equal, not as someone you are teaching.

The reason why presentations have become so popular can be summarised in one word – employability. Employers want staff who know the intricacies of their subject and at the same time are able to communicate their ideas in plain English to both expert and general audiences. The ability to deliver a good presentation is now essential if you are to build a successful career. Why? Because presentations are now part of most selection processes. By using presentations as a form of assessment, universities are preparing students for the needs of employers.

 Remember: Because most Masters programmes are assessed using assignments and not by examination, the effort you put in will be reflected in the mark you achieve. There is little or no element of luck involved as there is in closed-book examinations.

9.2 Delivering a great presentation

 Key point: The golden rule of any presentation is to be yourself. Don't try to be something you're not.

The danger for many people with an education background is that they think a presentation is really just a lesson by another name. Nothing could be further from the truth. The aim of a presentation is to provide information. It is then up to the individual members of the audience to decide what they wish to take from it. Presentations are didactic and presenter centred. And, unlike a lesson there is very little attempt to measure what the audience have learnt.

What follows are 15 points that you should take into account when designing and delivering a presentation at Masters level.

Be one of the first three to present. If a number of students are going to give presentations on the same day, volunteer to present first. As I keep saying, tutors are human and after watching six MA presentations, their attention and interest starts to wander (see 6.4) no matter how professional they are. So get in while the tutor is still fresh, bright-eyed, conscious and retains some will to live.

Know what criteria you will be marked against. You can find the criteria you will be judged against in the student or module handbook. Read it carefully and make sure that you cover all the points. However, a good presentation is about more than just covering the criteria. You can achieve that and still find that half your audience have fallen asleep and the other half are looking around for a sharp instrument to end their misery. You are dealing with human beings and they want to be entertained, intrigued, interested in and impressed by what you have to say. And that includes your tutor. Therefore, go beyond delivering just the 'criteria' facts and seek to engage your audience.

Know your audience. To engage your audience you have to know something about them. How well-disposed are they going to be towards you? Will they be friendly or hostile? What do they know about the subject? How interested are they likely to be in what you have to say? Why are they there? Yes, your tutor is there to assess your work, but what about the others in the audience, such as other tutors and/or students? How they react to your presentation can influence your tutor. Are they colleagues or strangers? Do they expect a formal presentation or a lively and possibly humorous event? Basically, the more you know about your audience the better, as it will enable you to meet and exceed their expectations.

 Warning: In any presentation you may well be speaking to an audience, some of whom may know more about the subject than you do. So never speak down to them.

Double-check the length of the presentation. Again, a statement of the obvious. The shorter the presentation the less detail you can go into. So identify the key high-level themes that you want to get across to your audience. The detail can go in a handout. Don't do as one student of mine did and turn up with 22 pages of closely typed material which they then tried to squeeze into a 20-minute presentation. With short presentations, any attempt to go into depth will confuse your audience and leave them feeing dissatisfied. It's better to get across three to five good solid points than rush through 15 which no one can remember.

Structure your presentation into three parts. Use the old teaching adage – tell them what you are going to tell them, tell them and finish by telling them what you told them. This is exactly what you do in an essay, where the introduction says what you are going to cover, the main body of the essay deals with the key issues you want to discuss and the conclusion summarises what you've written and highlights the key points.

Starting to plan. Once you know how long you have available, start to prepare the slides or other materials you are going to use. Practice in front of the mirror and time yourself. You can then add in or take out bits depending on the time it takes to deliver the core presentation.

Hint: It is the key points in your core presentation that you must get across at all costs – never cut that. Cut the time for questions if you have to, but not your core presentation.

Taking questions during a presentation can add significantly to the running time and it's impossible to estimate how much time they will take up. Therefore, tell people during the introduction that you will take questions at the end.

Hint: Depending on how confident you are about responding to questions, you can plan your presentation to leave a little or virtually no time for questions. You can then say with the sincerity of the average politician, 'I seem to have overrun slightly but I think I can take one, maybe two, questions'.

Illustrating your presentation. You can use PowerPoint. However, people are fed up with unimaginative PowerPoint presentations. Life's too short to live through another one. Consider using artefacts, film clips from the Internet, samples, models or pictures of what you are talking about. Always think 'What is the most effective resource that I can use? What will capture the audience's attention/imagination?' One of my students, who taught ancient history, brought in replicas of the tools that the ancient Egyptians used to extract the heart, brain and other vital organs before mummification. Now that was an effective and memorable presentation.

Hint: Every presentation should have one or two memorable moments/points. Identify yours and emphasise them.

Check your equipment. There is a saying in show business: 'Never work with children or animals'. In teaching, that becomes never rely on any equipment, such as a computer, laptop or white board that you intend to use, without checking that (a) it's available at the venue, (b) it's in working order and (c) you know how to use it – which includes knowing any passwords that you require. But even that is not enough. You also need a backup plan in case things go pear-shaped. Think about what you will do if you are left with a roomful of people and no mechanical or electrical resources. You may never need to use your backup plan but its very existence will increase your confidence and reduce your nerves.

 Warning: There is also a tradition in the theatre that actors need to check their clothing before stepping on stage. Male or female, you should do the same. Check that there are no costume malfunctions before you go on. You don't want the audience distracted!

Check out the venue. If possible, visit the room in advance where the presentation will take place. Look at the size of the room, the layout of the furniture and if you will be wearing a microphone or using a fixed mic. This information will determine how loudly you need to speak. Try it out for acoustics and remember that a room full of people will absorb sound in a way that an empty room does not.

Pitch the presentation at the right level. Consider the type of language you are going to use. Even with a Masters presentation you need to consider how much your audience knows about your pet subject. Yes, your tutor will know about it, but they will want to see if you can communicate your ideas to an audience with less-expert knowledge – your fellow students. Will they understand if you use technical terms and jargon?

Avoid reading from a script. I've seen this done at international conferences and I think it looks and sounds awful. Even if the speaker memorises the script and uses no notes it still comes out sounding like a speech, and a presentation is not a speech. If the subject matter is so complex that you have to read it, then it's too complex to be understood by a room-ful of listeners. Instead, give them a copy of your 'script' as a handout and just present the highlights as part of the presentation.

The three best ways to give a presentation are in:

- Third place: Speak from a set of fairly detailed notes, reading directly from them on occasion but also ad-libbing and maintaining eye contact with the group at other times.
- Second place: Use a set of skeleton notes as a guide and structure for your presentation, referring to them as required to keep you on track.
- First place: Use the PowerPoint slides, pictures, resources, models or whatever else you have as a series of props on which to hang your presentation. Then talk about and expand on each prop as appropriate, depending on the feedback you get from your audience and the time available. This last approach enables you to communicate with and respond to the audience and not just speak at them.

Speak clearly. Ensure that you can be heard by everyone in the room.

Look at your audience and maintain roving eye contact with different members of the audience as you speak. This will draw the audience in to you.

 Hint: Vary the tone of your voice and speed of delivery. Remember to hesitate after any word, phrase or idea that you wish to emphasise.

Monitor the audience. Throughout the presentation watch the audience; read their faces and body language. Check if they are restless or engaged, leaning forward listening or slumped down in their chairs, eyes closed. If you pick up that they are restless, do something to pull them back in. This can be difficult, but you can try changing the direction of your presentation, asking a question of the audience, changing the tone or speed of your delivery or moving closer to the audience and holding eye contact with more people.

Make a good first impression. It is still true that people form an opinion of you within the first two minutes of meeting/seeing you. So start your presentation with plenty of energy but don't fidget or rock from foot to foot. It will make you look nervous. Plant yourself on the platform and exude confidence, especially if you are feeling terrified. Use a friendly, conversational tone, speak clearly and make sure that your voice carries to all corners of the room. Your delivery shouldn't be too fast or too slow, and whatever you do, don't preach or talk down to your audience.

9.3 Twelve things not to do when making a presentation

Alas, it's not sufficient just to do certain things to create a great presentation – there are also some no no's that will kill any presentation stone dead no matter how well you have covered the issues in 9.2 above. These include the following don'ts:

- Apologise to the audience for your poor public speaking skills.
- Tell a joke to 'break the ice'.
- Speak too slowly or too quickly
- Speak too quietly or too loudly.
- Mumble or 'er' and 'um' throughout the presentation.
- Speak down to the audience or use unintelligible phrases or words.
- Avoid eye contact with the audience.
- Hop from foot to foot or pace up and down – both practices reveal your nervousness to the audience.
- Spend the entire presentation reading from your notes.
- Be over-serious. Keep the tone light and professional.
- Be afraid to say 'I don't know the answer to that question but I'll find out for you'.
- Overrun.

SPACE FOR YOUR NOTES

9.4 Essays

 Key point: As stated in 1.2, very few people who actually submit an assignment at Masters level fail. This section provides further advice on how you can virtually eliminate that risk.

I'm not going to repeat the advice given in Chapters 1, 4 and 5 about writing skills. If you've forgotten what was said now is a good time to review what was said. Instead I will provide specific advice on writing essays.

 Warning: Much of what I cover will be 'old news' to you. It's included because many Masters students seem to forget everything they were told about writing an essay when they start their first Masters assignment.

The reasons people fail essay assignments are legion but the three most common faults are:

- Failure to read the assignment brief and follow the instructions given. The result is that they answer the question they think has been set or wish had been set rather than the question that was set. Spend time reading the brief. If there is anything unclear or doubtful, speak to your tutor. Do not rely on what other students think. They are just as likely to be wrong as you are.
- Failing to heed the written or verbal advice given by the module tutor. Increasingly, universities issue a briefing paper to accompany each assignment. It reduces the number of students claiming that they weren't properly briefed about what was required. Again, if you don't understand the brief speak to your module tutor. Don't go to a different tutor, one you particularly like or the course director. They will not have the same detailed knowledge about what is required as the person who wrote the brief and who will mark your assignment. Whilst all tutors on a programme should have an understanding of all the modules, only the module leader

and those personally involved in teaching the module will fully understand all the nuances of the assignment, so ask them.

- The most common reason for failing is that the assignment isn't clear. Which is why getting a critical friend to read your work is so important (see 1.2 and 4.9). A good critical friend is invaluable. You want them to be frank with you and not tell you how wonderful you are.

Analyse your assignment question and identify keywords in an assignment brief. Even if you think you know what you have to do there is always the risk that your understanding is faulty. One way to minimise this error is to identify the keywords in any question. For example, the question 'Compare and contrast three theories of learning, illustrating your answer with examples from your practice' requires you to do three things. First, you are required to compare and contrast theories. Compare and contrast are process words and they describe what you have to do. If you analyse when you should be comparing and contrasting you may not fail your assignment but your marks will suffer because your assignment will lack the focus required for an excellent pass. See Handout 9.1 for the definition of common process words used in essays. Second, you are required to discuss three theories. Not two or four, but three. Third, you have to illustrate your answer with examples from your own practice.

Do this sort of analysis with every question you are given. If you are in doubt about anything ask your module tutor for clarification.

Engage with the task from day one. For best results, start to analyse any assignment questions when they are given to you, not the day before you start to write your essay. In most universities tutors will run an introduction to the module (module launch) and at that the assessment task will be explained. This is the time to consider the different aspects of the assignment and plan your way through it; after all, you don't want to miss important opportunities to gather relevant evidence from the lectures you'll be attending and the literature you will (hopefully) be reading. So begin to plan the assignment from the start of the module and be prepared to change the plan as time goes on and new aspects are introduced in the taught session.

Warning: Where you are given the title of your assignment at the start of the module, it is possible to start planning immediately. Compare this to the situation where you have to identify a topic to write about and how this requires you to wait before starting to plan your assignment (see 1.2).

Use mind maps or **spray diagrams** to plan your assignment. Both can help you to relate different topics to the original idea and each other. Being a fully paid up member of the Luddite Fraternity I like to draft my mind maps by hand. A piece of A3 paper works well.

Although, you may wish to use one of the many programs available to draft yours on a tablet or laptop.

The first two bubbles on any mind map should contain details of the positive and negative feedback you have received on previous assignments. I'm constantly amazed at how few students read the marker's comments. All they are interested in is the mark awarded. Unless you read and act upon your tutor's advice, how are you going to identify and rectify systemic and reoccurring errors in your work and build on the strengths that your tutors have identified in previous assignments?

Consider colour-coding different parts of the map or diagram to show which aspect of the assignment they relate to, e.g. introduction, discussion and conclusion.

For those who aren't so keen on mind maps and prefer a written plan, keep a reflective journal and include in it your ideas for the assignment as they arise. Never assume that you will remember a great idea you had for your assignment. From my experience I can categorically tell you that I have forgotten enough great ideas to write ten bestsellers. So write down your ideas immediately, even if it's on a dirty old scrap of paper.

Finding literature for your assignment. Your tutor/marker will want to see evidence that you have researched the topic above and beyond the few books and articles on the reading list. Read chapter sections 5.1 to 5.7 again. Everything I said in those sections applies just as much to essays as research reports, dissertations and writing in the style of a journal article.

 Warning: For some reason, students often apply less critical evaluation to the literature they use in essays than when writing up a piece of research. Just because it's an essay doesn't mean that you can be any less critical of the material you use.

Structure your essay. You will be more familiar with writing essays than research reports and dissertations. Despite that, I would ask you to keep in mind the following two pieces of advice which were old when Adam was still a schoolboy.

 Hint: A good essay should contain an introduction, five good points that relate to the question and a conclusion.

 Hint: In any essay, start by telling the reader what the essay is about. Then tell them in detail what you have to say on the subject and end by telling them what you have said.

From the above it's clear that most essays have three sections, namely, an introduction, a discussion and a conclusion.

The introduction sets the scene for the assignment, what it's going to be about, why it's important and how the rest of the assignment is structured (see Handout 8.1).

The discussion, or main body, of the essay is where your arguments are developed and you draw on the literature you have collected to support, explore, analyse and refute the various ideas discussed. While it is common in essays to put forward your own arguments, it's essential that you support your views with reference to published literature/research.

The conclusion should draw your arguments together and summarise the key points. No new material should be introduced at this stage. Use the rule of three when writing your conclusion. List and discuss the three most important things you have learnt, any weaknesses in what you have written and how you would avoid the same problems in future. End by outlining any further work that you might undertake to improve your understanding of the issues discussed.

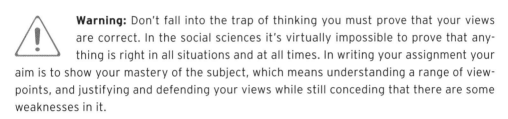 **Warning:** Don't fall into the trap of thinking you must prove that your views are correct. In the social sciences it's virtually impossible to prove that anything is right in all situations and at all times. In writing your assignment your aim is to show your mastery of the subject, which means understanding a range of viewpoints, and justifying and defending your views while still conceding that there are some weaknesses in it.

SPACE FOR YOUR NOTES

9.5 Writing your assignment

Much of the advice that would normally appear here has already been covered in 4.1 to 4.11 and 8.1 to 8.10. I don't propose to revisit that material here. Rather, I just wish to emphasise a few points.

The assignment you hand in must be logically structured, but the order in which you write your essay is unimportant. A surprising number of professional writers write the ending first, and I don't mean 'The End'. You can start anywhere you like. Just like building a jigsaw, you can fill in whichever part of the picture you want to first. You can move the various sections around at a later stage to produce the structure your tutor expects.

Develop your own way of writing/writing habits. How you go about writing your assignment doesn't matter. If you can only write your first draft long-hand then do that. If you can only write in the evening or morning, then do that. If you can only write while wearing your favourite onesie then wear it (but not in the library, please). All that matters is that you produce as good an assignment as you can within the timescale allowed.

Always keep in mind the audience you're writing for and the reason why you are writing the assignment. Don't fall into the trap of thinking that because you're writing for your tutor you don't need to explain the jargon, theories and key terms that you use. Yes, he or she will already know them. But what they want to see is that you also know them, and the only way you can demonstrate this is by writing about them.

Remember the ABCs of good writing. Aim for accuracy, brevity and, above all, clarity in everything you write (see 4.5 to 4.7). Don't use long words for the sake of it and avoid colloquialisms and non-professional language such as 'I think that the humanistic school is "great" or "wicked"'. Such language weakens your argument and we poor ancient tutors may not even understand them! It's also inappropriate and out of place and makes you sound like a complete (fill in your own descriptor here).

Aim to make your assignment pleasant and interesting to read; after all, your tutor will be marking a lot of the same assignments and the easier you make it for them the better. Use transitions to link sentences, paragraphs and sections, such as 'Having discussed X, I will now consider Y'. Use the process words from the assignment too; for example, 'having discussed the strengths of the cognitive school, I will now consider the weaknesses'. Provide a roadmap for the reader. Tell the person marking the work what you have done and will do; convince them that you have answered the question.

Check and check again. As with any piece of written work when you have finished ask your critical friend or the AST to read it through and identify any errors.

 Remember: You don't have to take the advice given by student support or your critical friend. You know more about your assignment and what you are trying to achieve with it than anyone else. It's your assignment and ultimately your responsibility. So make your own decision – but don't reject a point simply because you are stung by the criticism that it implies.

As a final check, go back and read through your assignment one last time. Read it aloud and listen for 'the errors'. Then check that you have referenced all material correctly. Quotations should only be used when the form of words is important and the message would be weakened by putting it any other way. Don't produce an assignment that is little more than a series of linked quotes. The key is to put ideas in your own words when possible and to make sure that you fully reference the original (see 5.10).

9.6 Check that you've followed all the rules

Universities are pernickety and if you don't follow the rules to the letter you can lose marks, that is:

- Stay within the word limit. If you have to cut, see what material can be moved to the appendices. If you're still over, look for paragraphs, sentences and single words that you can delete without weakening your argument/assignment. There is always some fat that can be cut! Undertake this exercise with a copy of the assignment criteria beside you and tick off each aspect of the criteria as you read your assignment.
- Submit your assignment on time. If it's 13.00 hours don't file it at 13.05. Submissions are usually time-stamped and if you submit late you will either lose marks or find that your assignment has been failed. Think of the deadline as that moment in an exam when the invigilator says 'Put your pen down'. If you continue writing after that you would expect to be reprimanded.
- Submit your assignment in the right format. Does the university want a soft copy, a hard copy or both?
- Follow the guidelines as regards acceptable fonts and required font size and spacing. As a general rule, always double-space your assignment and use either Times New Roman or Arial with font size 12.
- Check submission requirements such as the need for spiral binding and the number of copies required.

9.7 Conclusion

Don't be afraid of presentations. Have the confidence to take control of the presentation. That way you can decide how much interaction you'll allow with the audience during and at the end of the presentation. Learn your lines like a good 'actor' – turn up and perform. And if you are asked a question that you can't answer don't be worried about saying 'I don't know. But I'll find out and get back to you'. Admitting that you don't know is a sign of strength, not weakness. Weakness is trying to bamboozle the audience with an answer that you just dreamed up and you know is wrong.

Essays should be your friend. If you have a first degree in an arts or social science subject the chances are that you've written hundreds of essays over the years. The only thing you need to remember is that you are now writing at Masters level and anything which is just 'good enough' isn't good enough at Masters level. If you're not stretching yourself and producing the best work you can, you're not working hard enough.

SPACE FOR YOUR NOTES

Further reading

Bailey, S. (2011) *Academic Writing: A Handbook for International Students* (3rd ed.). Abingdon: Routledge.
McGrath, J. and Coles, A. (2013) *Your Education Research Project Companion* (2nd ed.). Abingdon: Routledge.
McGrath, J. and Coles, A. (2016) *Your Teacher Training Companion* (2nd ed.). Abingdon: Routledge.
Wilkinson, D. (2005) *The Essential Guide to Postgraduate Study*. London: SAGE.

HANDOUT 9.1 Process words used in assignment questions

Analyse	Break the subject down into its different parts – then explain how the parts are connected to each other.
Compare	Summarise both similarities and differences between ideas or concepts.
Contrast	Identify the distinctive features between two or more concepts.
Critique	Make a judgement based on the available evidence.
Define	State the exact meaning of words or phrases.
Describe	Provide an account of a topic based on available facts.
Discuss	Debate the relative merits of an idea or concept by identifying its strengths and weaknesses.
Evaluate	Arrive at a judgement on the value of an idea or concept.
Examine	Describe the material or data in great detail.
Explain	Give a detailed account of the reasons for a particular phenomenon.
Illustrate	Use examples to clarify an idea, often supported by reference to pictures, diagrams or charts.
Interpret	Provide an explanation for something based on available evidence.
Justify	Seek to show that a claim made by you or another author is reasonable given the evidence available.
List/ enumerate	Provide a series of statements concerning the phenomena under review.
Relate	Show how the issues under discussion are connected to another set of issues/ideas.
Summarise	Provide a summary of the main points in sequence without going into detail.

10 Where next?

> **Aim of chapter:** To explore some of the options available to you on completion of your Masters.
>
> **Chapter overview:** This chapter outlines the options available to a student who has recently completed their Masters in Education. Options are discussed under four headings: career advancement, including work in the private sector; opportunities for self-employment; undertaking further study at undergraduate, Masters or Doctoral level; and continuous professional development.

10.1 Introduction

 Key point: One stage of your life ends when you get a Masters degree and another opens up. Have the courage to grab your new life with both hands.

It's very easy for your Masters studies to take over your life. Indeed there is good research evidence that advanced study can lead to a breakdown in pre-existing relationships. This can be caused by a number of factors: the student's changing attitudes to life, re-evaluation of lifestyle and goals, new relationships forged at the university or their partner finding someone else because they feel excluded from their partner's new life. These are just a few of the problems that can arise.

Even if the problem isn't as severe as the above, you need to brush up on your relationships with partners, family and friends. So before you start on any new project, take a year off to make a fuss of those you love and care for and to recharge your own batteries. That doesn't mean that it needs be a fallow year. Use this quiet time to assess what you want to do and where you want to go next.

Basically there are three avenues you can follow. You can use your Masters to:

- advance your career;
- become self-employed;
- continue your studies.

10.2 Advancing your career

The world will not suddenly become your oyster, lobster or octopus just because you have obtained a Masters qualification. But it will open doors for you. Once through the door, the amount of effort you put into your studies and how much you have developed personally and intellectually during your studies will determine how well equipped you are to grasp these new opportunities.

Increasingly the British Government is looking to promote the title Chartered Teacher as a way of identifying and rewarding the best-qualified teachers. The idea is that the great teachers will no longer have to desert the classroom and become school managers and leaders to obtain a higher salary and increased status. Achieving Chartered status will bring both. Current thinking seems to be, and this could change, that Chartered status would be awarded to those who hold a Masters-level qualification. Which is, of course, a partial return to the situation when holding a Masters qualification was recognition that you were qualified to teach (see 2.4).

Some teaching posts are already asking applicants for a Masters-level qualification, e.g. a PGCE with all modules at Masters level. But this still remains relatively rare. Heads continue to want good teachers, not people who are great students – the two are different! What is more likely to happen is that when an organisation finds that it has 20-plus applicants who have all met the essential list of requirements they turn to the desirable requirements to act as a sort of tie-break between candidates. Often one of the desirable characteristics listed is possession of a Masters or similar level qualification. This enables employers to select six to eight people to interview on objective grounds and therefore avoid any criticism about unfair selection and recruitment policies.

If you are applying for a management post, either internally or externally, you may find that holding a Masters qualification, or equivalent, is an essential criteria. What can be considered equivalent can vary from organisation to organisation but will almost certainly include some of the qualifications offered by the National College for Teaching and Leadership.

 Hint: If you wish to advance to Head of Year, Assistant Head, Deputy or Head, a Masters qualification will definitely be an advantage, particularly if you studied one or more modules dealing with management and leadership as part of your course.

Your Masters may also open doors in the private sector. Don't be afraid of applying. As someone who has worked in both the public and private sectors I can confirm that both have their fair share of geniuses, hardworking staff, idiots and morons.

With your Masters tucked under your arm, the private sector offers you opportunities to become involved in a wide range of consultancy projects as well as staff training and development in the education sector. Such experience will stand you in good stead should you ever wish to return to education and become a Head or run an academy or free school.

10.3 Opportunities for self-employment

You may, of course, decide to become self-employed following completion of your Masters. I have known many students who used their Masters to start their own training company or consultancy. The challenges and rewards that such a move can bring are outside the scope of this book, but if you are willing to launch your own organisation the initials MA offer a recognition factor that few qualifications can match and will provide you with a competitive advantage.

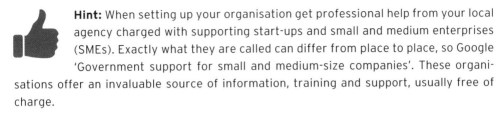

Hint: When setting up your organisation get professional help from your local agency charged with supporting start-ups and small and medium enterprises (SMEs). Exactly what they are called can differ from place to place, so Google 'Government support for small and medium-size companies'. These organisations offer an invaluable source of information, training and support, usually free of charge.

Once you have the outlines of a business plan, speak to an accountant about your plan and business finance before you approach any bank for funding. It's essential to produce a sound business plan and the impression of a professional organisation to your bank. Appointing an accountant and solicitor, or at least naming your intended professionals, will aid this.

Hint: When you start off be prepared to do whatever is necessary to survive the first few hard years. While you are building a customer base and reputation, don't be too proud to do some visiting teaching/lecturing. Approach your old MA supervisor and see if they can use you for all or part of a module – that's how I got started in higher education.

SPACE FOR YOUR NOTES

10.4 Continue your studies

While there are many excellent one-off education and training courses available, if you are anything like me you will probably prefer a structured course that gives you another recognised qualification. Let's be honest, we all take a secret pride in the letters after our name.

It is entirely possible to continue your studies by taking another Masters course or even an undergraduate course for those who don't have a first degree. These options are neither a backward nor sideways step. They are often based on the mature reflection of an autonomous learner who has identified where they have weaknesses in their education and the best way to fill the gap. So don't rule them out.

Warning: When thinking about continuing your studies the assumption usually is that you do so at a higher level. In 2.6 I stated that there is not a significant step up from level 6 (last year of an undergraduate degree) to level 7 Masters. This is not true of the step up to level 8 Doctoral study. The gap is truly enormous. If you are a full-time student you will probably spend the first year trying to reach the required standard in terms of thinking and writing. If you are a part-time student it will take longer.

Your studies at Masters level will not prepare you for the shock of Doctoral studies, where you suddenly find that tutors who previously were highly supportive and positive about the quality of your work have now become the Grand Inquisitor Torquemada and suddenly question everything you write and ask that you support all claims fully. It's quite a culture shock. From being a confident Masters student you find yourself questioning everything you thought you knew about your specialist subject, along with your own attitudes, beliefs and bias. It's an uncomfortable and unsettling process. And it's supposed to be. Any good Doctoral experience will change your attitude to knowledge and life, your beliefs and you as a person. So don't say you haven't been warned.

On the plus side, a good Doctoral experience is also exciting, hugely enjoyable, interesting, rewarding and plain unmissable if you really want to test the limits of your academic and intellectual abilities.

But please don't run away with the idea that a doctorate is only for the elite. It's not. This will probably make me unpopular with some educationalists, but I think that you do need above-average intelligence to successfully complete a Ph.D. or an Ed.D. But you don't have to be a genius. There are a lot of geniuses out there who will tell you that they have completed their doctorate except for writing their thesis.

The major benefits that having a Masters qualification will give you at Doctoral level is that you will be familiar with writing literature reviews and undertaking small-scale research projects. These are valuable skills. When you start your doctorate you will probably think that you know everything you need to know about these areas (just as I did). But beware. You've been swimming in a heated pool – you're just about to be introduced to the Atlantic Ocean.

If I've not put you off, there are now two routes to a doctorate that you can follow: the Ed.D. and the Ph.D.

The professional doctorate: the Doctor of Education (Ed.D.) is ideal for teachers, trainers and lecturers who wish to research a subject of professional interest.

Each Ed.D. will have a named pathway, e.g. Ed.D. in Education Management and Leadership or Ed.D. in Education Psychology. You join a specified pathway and in the first two years attend a series of taught modules, including mandatory research training, submit assignments and work towards identifying a suitable topic for your thesis.

In the third and fourth years you are allocated a research supervisor and undertake your research and write up your thesis. All 360 credits at level 8 are normally attached solely to your thesis, as only your thesis is examined by viva. It's entirely possible for part-time students to complete the course in four years, but five may be a more reasonable target.

Key point: The great advantage of the Ed.D. is that students enjoy a structured learning framework while they come to terms with working at/towards Doctoral level. In addition, for the first two years of the course they enjoy regular taught sessions in the company of fellow students. In many ways these first two years are a bit like a Masters-plus course. There are now a number of Ph.D. programmes that are adopting a similar structure.

The academic doctorate: the Doctor of Philosophy (Ph.D.) has traditionally involved three years' full-time research and anything up to eight years' part-time study, at the end of which you are examined on your thesis at a viva. The Ph.D. is the preferred qualification for those who wish to make a career in higher education, academia or research, although holders of the Ed.D. are increasingly being found in these areas as well.

It is essential that there is someone at the university who is research-active in your area of interest. Details of the research interests for each member of staff are usually available online. Contact the appropriate person for an informal chat and only then submit your application, including an initial idea outline of about 1,000 words with your application form. You will then be interviewed.

If you are successful at interview, you will probably find that you are initially registered as an M.Phil. student even if you already have a Masters. Provided you show satisfactory progress during your first year full-time (two years part-time), you will be reregistered as a Ph.D. student.

In recent years 'new' Ph.D. formats have been trialed by universities, with some adopting an approach not that much different to the Ed.D. A range of titles have been devised to describe these 'New Ph.D.s' such as the 2+2 Ph.D. These 'non-traditional' courses are well worth a look, as the additional support/structure that many of them provide can be the difference between completing your studies and leaving the course disillusioned.

SPACE FOR YOUR NOTES

10.5 Continuous professional development (CPD)

If you decide to stay in the classroom, seek promotion, move to the private sector or set up your own business, it's essential that you continually update your professional knowledge. Continuous professional development ensures that you stay abreast of the latest developments in your profession and keeps you 'match fit' for those important interviews with prospective employers or clients.

Annually, you should use the analytical, evaluative and research skills that you learnt on your Masters to draw up a training needs analysis. Start by identifying the skills and knowledge that you already have. Then identify what areas you need to update and what new skills and information you need to acquire. Identify the gap between where you are at currently and where you want to be and develop a strategy to eliminate it. This might be achieved by attending a short training session or course, being mentored by a senior member of staff in your organisation or carrying out a small-scale piece of research devised by you to improve your own professional skills and knowledge. Or enrolling on another formal qualification.

 Remember: You, and the skills and knowledge that you have, are the greatest single asset you possess. Everything else flows from that – your job, car, house, etc. Therefore, never be afraid to invest time, energy and money in your own development.

10.6 Conclusion

You can feel lost and directionless when you finish your Masters. That's not a good state of mind to be in when making a decision about where you go next. Take the time to enjoy your success. Buy yourself a keepsake, a memento of your achievement, e.g. a watch, painting or maybe a new car. Something that you want and deserve following all your hard work. That way, every time you look at it you can feel proud that you achieved something that very few people ever do – you passed your MA.

Don't jump at the first opportunity that arises, be that a job or a new course. Instead, relax and enjoy a normal life for a while. Be kind to yourself. That way when you seriously start to consider your next step, you will do so with a clear and rested mind which now has the ability to analyse and critically evaluate the myriad of opportunities that are now available to you.

Good luck.

SPACE FOR YOUR NOTES

Further reading

Allison, S. (2014) *Perfect Teacher-Led CPD*. Carmarthen: Independent Thinking Press.

Glossary of terms

Some of the terms used in education and many of those used in education research have never been codified. This means that they vary, to some extent, from book to book. This can be confusing. The following glossary defines how each of the listed terms has been used in this book.

abstract A short summary of the research that you have undertaken which appears immediately after the title page.

action research A cyclical process concerned with continuous improvement in which the researcher seeks to improve their professional practice by implementing a series of small interventions and monitoring the impact that each has.

analysis The act of breaking down a theory or data into its component parts.

anonymity Ensuring that participants cannot be identified by removing their name or any data that might identify them from a research report (see confidentiality).

anti-positivist The philosophical belief that there is not one single discoverable reality but, instead, that every person builds for themselves their own reality based upon their experience and beliefs.

assessment criteria A series of graded statements, linked to the learning outcomes, against which the work of learners is judged.

audit trail The provision of sufficient information in the final research report for the reader to understand why, how and what the researcher did.

autonomous learner A learner who is capable of undertaking study with minimum guidance from their teacher or supervisor.

baseline data Data collected to establish what the current position is.

bias The effect of the researcher's or participants' predispositions on findings.

British Education Index (BEI) A specialised search engine usually available at http://www.leeds. ac.uk/bei, or at most university libraries, designed to search academic works in education.

case study A detailed description and analysis of a bounded instance/phenomenon using multiple data collection methods.

compact A written agreement between 2 or more people.

conceptual framework A conceptual framework is what a researcher constructs from the writing of others. It is the lens through which they view their work/research. It is used to explain, explore and challenge the data collected.

confidentiality Not reporting any data or information that a participant has specifically asked you to withhold (see anonymity).

critical evaluation Involves weighing the strengths and weaknesses of an argument using evidence from one's experience, collected data and/or the writing of others.

critical friend A peer in a similar position to you who provides non-judgemental feedback on academic work or professional practice.

deterministic Term used to describe how the norms of society control/determine how an individual acts.

didactic Teaching in an instructive manner, e.g. lectures and presentations in which learners/audience play a passive role.

Education Resources Information Center (ERIC) An American academic search engine for education sources. Available at http://www.eric.ed.gov or most university libraries.

empirical research Research involving data physically gathered by a researcher rather than the process of philosophical thought.

epistemology The theory of knowledge and what counts as valid knowledge.

ethics The social, moral and professional conventions and beliefs that underpin the basis upon which research should be carried out.

ethnography Research strategy that investigates in great detail the behaviour and culture of a group of people.

experiments A scientific process by which a hypothesis is confirmed or refuted.

feedback Feedback is the verbal or written response that a teacher provides to a learner on their performance with the intent to eliminate errors and improve future performance.

focal paragraph A paragraph or more that summarises the aims of the research.

focus The precise aspect of any phenomena that you wish to research.

generalisable The extent to which the findings from a piece of research will be found in all similar situations.

grounded theory A research approach involving the development of theory based upon the data collected.

hypothesis A prediction or supposition.

ideographic A research approach that focuses on the experiences of the individual.

informed consent The full, free and voluntary consent given by research participants when they agree to take part in research.

instance Term used to describe and help define the boundaries of a case study in terms of people, organisations, events or phenomena to be studied.

interpretivist research Term used to describe a range of research approaches that are anti-positivist in nature and deal with people's feelings, attitudes and beliefs.

intervention A change initiated as part of an action research project.

interviews A guided discussion with the intent of obtaining relevant information from the interviewee.

learner-centred A teaching style that focuses on the learner and what they are required to do.

Likert scale Usually a five-point scale used in questionnaires to evaluate strength of opinion for or against a statement.

mind maps See spray diagrams.

new university Those ex-polytechnics that were incorporated as universities under the Further and Higher Education Act 1992.

non-participant observation The observation of an event or process by an individual who takes no part in the proceedings.

observations A data collection method which involves watching what actually happens as opposed to what people say happened.

ontology The study of the nature of existence and the structure of reality.

paradigm A philosophical or theoretical framework. A way of thinking and organising ideas into a coherent pattern.

participant observation The observation of an event or process by someone who is taking part in the process as part of their everyday work.

peer review A process whereby academics review the work of other academics in the same field of study to determine if it is worthy of publication.

phenomenology An approach to studying the conscious experience of events from the perspective of the individual.

plagiarism The act of passing off someone else's work or idea as your own.

population The entire set or group from which the researcher can select.

positivist The philosophical belief that there is one discoverable reality.

primary data Raw or unprocessed data.

primary research Any research which involves the collection of original data from its source.

process words Words which tell you what you have to do in order to correctly answer a question.

professional journals Journals that publish articles of professional interest which are not peer-reviewed.

provenance The academic credibility of a source. This usually relates to whether an article has been peer-reviewed and the status of the writer and/or publisher.

qualified teacher status (QTS) The professional qualification required to teach in a school in England or Wales.

qualitative research Research that is concerned with the attitudes, beliefs, feelings, interpretations and perceptions of participants and understanding the realities that they inhabit.

quantitative research Research that is concerned with measurement of the phenomena under review and discovery of a single reality.

quasi-experiments Quasi-experimental design involves selecting groups, without using random selection, and then testing a variable within the selected group.

questionnaires A set of written questions issued to a selected group.

reading strategies Approaches taken to reading text, such as skim reading or only reading specific sections of the document, such as the executive summary.

realist One who believes that there is a single, discoverable reality.

red brick universities Those universities, such as the University of Birmingham and the University of Liverpool, that were built during the Victorian and Edwardian age and generally enjoy a very high academic reputation.

reflective journal A descriptive and evaluative record of the research progress.

relatable The degree to which aspects of findings in one location may be relevant to other situations.

reliability The degree to which the same results would be obtained if the research or experiment were repeated.

research A logical process using data and/or theory to increase the researcher's understanding of the phenomena under investigation.

research focus A statement which specifies clearly which aspects of the phenomena are to be investigated.

research methodology A term used to describe the entire approach adopted by the researcher or just the philosophy that underpins the work, e.g. a quantitative or qualitative methodology.

research questions A series of statements specifying precisely what the researcher hopes to discover more about.

research strategy The framing structure into which the research methods used fit, e.g. action research, case studies and surveys.

research tools Sometimes called 'research instruments'. These are the resources used to gather data, such as a questionnaire, interview schedule or observation schedule.

Russell Group universities A group of 24 research-active universities that enjoy a very high academic reputation. The group includes Oxford and Cambridge, as well as many red brick universities.

sample That part of the entire population selected to take part in the research.

secondary data Processed data, such as percentages, obtained from raw data or data extracted from previously published material.

secondary research Research that is undertaken using data obtained from other sources or is based upon the reading of literature only.

semi-structured interviews A structured conversation where open-ended questions are used to explore the interviewee's opinions on a series of issues, and digression is limited.

seminal works A book or article that continues to be of fundamental importance to a field of study, regardless of its age. Your work would be incomplete without quoting this source.

spray diagram/mind map Diagram showing the interconnections and relationships between ideas, theories and issues.

standards Statements related to expected performance criteria – in this case related to study at Masters level.

structured interviews An interview in which most/all of the questions are closed and the respondent has little chance to digress from the interviewer's agenda.

subjectivist The doctrine that all knowledge is limited by a person's individual experience.

subvocalisation 'Hearing' words in the mind when reading without speaking them aloud.

survey The collection of data from a large number of participants, usually at a single point in time, with the intention of establishing what the current situation is.

synthesis The process of taking the component parts of a theory or data obtained from analysis, and reassembling the parts into something new and/or different.

teacher-centred A teaching style that focuses on what the teacher does rather than the actions of the learners.

theoretical framework A theoretical framework is a collection of interconnected concepts, ideas and theories that a researcher constructs in their literature review and then uses it to analyse, challenge, evaluate, interrogate, support or refute the data she or he has collected.

triangulation The use of two or more methodologies, methods, researchers, categories of respondent, or time periods with the intention of gaining a clear picture of the phenomenon under review.

unstructured interviews An interview in which the researcher asks very open-ended questions and leaves the choice of what information to give to the interviewee. An unstructured interview provides the respondent with the greatest leeway in how to respond to questions that are open, non-specific and wide in scope.

validity The degree to which the research has measured/explored the phenomena that it set out to study.

variables The component parts that exist and are at play in any social situation or experiment.

viva voce A verbal examination.

References

Allison, S. (2014) *Perfect Teacher-Led CPD*. Carmarthen: Independent Thinking Press.

Bailey, S. (2011) *Academic Writing: A Handbook for International Students* (3rd ed.). Abingdon: Routledge.

Biggam, J. (2011) *Succeeding with Your Masters Dissertation: A Step-by-Step Handbook* (2nd ed.). Berkshire: OUP/McGraw-Hill.

British Educational Research Association, ‹www.bera.ac.uk›, accessed 25 Oct. 2014.

Cohen, L., Manion, L. and Morrison, K. (2011) *Research Methods in Education* (7th ed.). Abingdon: Routledge.

Compare different qualifications, ‹www.gov.uk/what-different-qualification-levels-mean/overview›, accessed 1 Feb. 2015.

Denscombe, M. (2014) *The Good Research Guide: For Small-Scale Research Projects* (5th ed.). Berkshire: OUP/McGraw-Hill.

Glaser, B. and Strauss, A. (1967) *The Discovery of Grounded Theory: Strategies for Qualitative Research*. New York: Aldine de Gruyter.

McGivney, V. (1993) Participation and Non-Participation: A Review of the Literature, in Edwards, R., Sieminski, S. and Zeldin, D. (Eds) *Adult Learners, Education and Training: A Reader*. London: Routledge/OUP.

McGrath, J. and Coles, A. (2013) *Your Education Research Project Companion* (2nd ed.). Abingdon: Routledge.

McGrath, J. and Coles, A. (2016) *Your Teacher Training Companion* (2nd ed.). Abingdon: Routledge.

Office of Qualifications and Examinations Regulation (Ofqual), ‹www.ofqual.gov.uk›, accessed 25 Oct. 2014.

Pring, R. (2003) Different Kinds of Research and Their Philosophical Foundations, in *Philosophy of Educational Research*. London: Continuum.

Ridley, D. (2012) *The Literature Review: A Step-by-Step Guide for Students*. London: SAGE.

Strauss, A. and Corbin, J. (1990) *Basics of Qualitative Research: Grounded Theory, Procedures, and Techniques*. London: SAGE.

Wilkinson, D. (2005) *The Essential Guide to Postgraduate Study*. London: SAGE.

Willis, P. (2000) *Learning to Labour: How Working Class Kids Get Working Class Jobs*. Farnham: Ashgate Publishing.

Index